To a dear
friend in kind since
Christ — may these
pages may of grace,
strength and grace,
that will be of real help,
to your life of real,
Love always,
Joy

ON BEING
A REAL CHRISTIAN

Gilbert L Purtee

ON BEING
A REAL CHRISTIAN

by

G. CHRISTIAN WEISS

Author of *The Perfect Will of God*

MOODY PRESS
CHICAGO

CONTENTS

FOREWORD

When a baby comes to bless a home, the parents take precautions to protect him from disease and accident. They make every effort to give the child a properly balanced diet, so that he will have a good start in life and will thus have a healthy, strong body when he is grown.

In a truly Christian home the parents will be careful to indoctrinate the child properly in spiritual matters and fortify him for later years.

So often, however, a newborn babe in Christ is taken for granted. Older, more mature Christians fail to see the need of protecting him from possible pitfalls. They do not recognize the necessity of proper foundation training in important Christian doctrines and practices.

"On Being a Real Christian" is designed partially to meet the need of a new Christian. Mr. Weiss, director of the Gospel Missionary Union, has given much diligence to the preparation of this treatise. We feel that great benefit can be derived if this book is placed in the hands of new Christians and if they will read it and carefully apply the suggestions that have been set forth.

Mr. Weiss is well qualified to give such advice. He not only has a family of his own, but as the director of the Gospel Missionary Union, with headquarters in Kansas City, Missouri, he has been able to analyze the need of young Christians. Here he has given us in written form many of the principles which he has put into practice over a period of years.

Pastors, Christian workers, and evangelists will find this book invaluable in working with babes in Christ. We recommend it highly and trust that it will have a wide circulation.

—Theodore H. Epp

CHAPTER I

SALVATION—GOD'S SIDE

The first fact that every person must face as he ponders his spiritual relationship to God is that of SIN. Every human being is conscious of sin, to some extent, although some may not want to admit it openly. When a person wants to pray or turn to God in time of need, almost immediately that innate consciousness of sin and unworthiness looms up within him. How can one who is so full of sin gain an audience with God? How can such a one experience fellowship with a Holy God? These are the first questions that invade the mind of the seeking soul.

The consciousness of sin is not merely the result of childhood training, nor does it come only to those who read and know the Bible. Even in heathen lands men and women have that same inner consciousness of sin when they desire to approach God. The religion of the heathen is characterized by its unceasing attempt to atone for sin and to appease the displeasure of God. Heathen altars are quite universally stained with the blood of animals or of humans. This is because mankind is universally conscious of sin.

Concerning the heathen, who are in darkness as to the Bible and Christian truth, the Apostle Paul says, "Which shew the work of the law written in their hearts, their conscience also bearing witness, and their thoughts the mean while accusing or else excusing one another" (Rom. 2:15).

You, too, must, or already have, come face to face with this unalterable fact of sin. As you come to consider the matter of your salvation and reconciliation with God, you become terribly conscious of that wall of sin that stands between you and God as an insurmountable barrier. Your conscience tells you that you have sinned. Common honesty tells you that you have sinned. The convicting voice of God's Spirit tells you that you have sinned. Above all, the Bible tells you that you have sinned. "All have sinned," it declares, "and come short of the glory of God" (Rom. 3:23). "There is none righteous, no, not one" (Rom. 3:10). "All we like sheep have gone astray; we have turned every one to his own way" (Isa. 53:6). The Bible's testimony against our sins is universal, indicting, and indisputable. WE HAVE SINNED. WE ARE SINNERS. In this group you, along with all the rest of the human family, must take your place.

Over against this consciousness of sin there also arises within the human heart a corresponding consciousness of the holiness and justice of God. God is pure and holy, by common consent. God is righteous. God must be just; therefore, He cannot countenance or tolerate sin. If He could, He would not be God, for a God who winked at wickedness could never meet the necessary attributes of deity. This we all realize.

A good judge in a legal court must punish all wrongdoing. If he does not do so, he will soon be removed from his bench. A judge must judge; he cannot by-pass judgment. He dare not forgive and exonerate any guilty person. His position as a justice, in our highest conception of law, does not permit him to do so. He might cherish a deep, inner desire to exonerate the guilty man at his bar, but he cannot, under any circumstances, do so. No matter how much compassion and pity he might feel toward the culprit, he cannot exercise it, for justice must prevail. So it is with the great, just Judge above and the sinful human race. Divine justice cannot permit the guilt of human sin to be ignored.

That God loves men, though they are sinful, is also beyond dispute. The love of God is one of the main themes of Scripture. God loves the entire human race—every son of Adam. God loves you by virtue of the single fact that you are human. Nothing else is required to qualify you for a place in His love. When you can count on nothing else in the whole world, you can count on the love of God. When all human loves have become exhausted or have been withdrawn, you can still rest on the fact that God loves you.

There is really no room to doubt this, dear friend. The Bible says, "God so loved the world, that he gave his only begotten Son" (John 3:16). "God commendeth his love toward us, in that, while we were yet sinners, Christ died for us" (Rom. 5:8). "I have loved thee with an everlasting love" (Jer. 31:3). "When my father and my mother forsake me, then the Lord will take me up" (Ps. 27:10). The love of God for sinning men is beautifully illustrated by Christ in the parable of the Prodigal Son, found in the fifteenth chapter of the Gospel of Luke. Although this son had wandered far away and had fallen deep into sin, the father loved him still and received him again with tears of joy and the kiss of forgiveness.

God is, furthermore, most certainly a God of mercy. Mercy and love always go together. There can never be one without the other. As love dwells in God, likewise does mercy—boundless, endless mercy. The Psalmist exclaimed, "His mercy is from everlasting to everlasting!" Mercy desires always to forgive and never to punish. Mercy ever pleads for leniency, for exoneration, for pardon, and for exemption from penalty for the guilty soul.

God is both a God of justice and a God of mercy. But how can He exercise both in dealing with sinners? Justice requires that our sins be punished. Yet God's own love pleads for the sinner's pardon. How can He do both? How could He both punish and pardon sin? How should He deal with us? How could He be both just and merciful to us who are so full of sin? How could He solve the great problem of our salvation?

Thank God, He has yet another divine attribute—WISDOM. In His infinite wisdom, stimulated by His holy love, God solved this great problem and provided a way for our salvation. The divine answer to the problem of the salvation of sinners was THE CROSS. On the cross His own divine, beloved Son died in the place of guilty sinners, paying in full the penalty of their sins, thus providing a way of salvation for all. At the cross justice is satisfied, for there sin was fully penalized. There on that cross, Christ, being infinite, paid the infinite penalty required by divine justice for our sins. Sin was not winked at —it was punished. "The Lord hath laid on him the iniquity of us all" (Isa. 53.6). "Christ died for our sins" (I Cor. 15:3). "Christ . . . suffered for sins, the just for the unjust, that he might bring us to God" (I Pet. 3:18). "His own self bare our sins in his own body on the tree" (I Pet. 2:24). When He died, some of His last words were, "It is finished." What did He mean? He meant that atonement for men's sins was finished. Justice was satisfied. The price was paid. Mercy can now be extended to sinful beings!

Thus we see at the cross that both God's justice and His mercy are operative—and both are requited. His holiness, which required the just punishment of sin, was satisfied, and His mercy, which cried for man's pardon, was also satisfied. It is little wonder that Paul said of the cross that it is "the power of God, and the wisdom of God" (I Cor. 1:24). Only the infinite wisdom of God could have devised such a wondrous and perfect plan of redemption. Contemplating this, William R. Newell wrote:

> O, the love that drew salvation's plan!
> O, the grace that brought it down to man!
> O, the mighty gulf that God did span
> At Calvary!

Only the cross could be the answer for our salvation. The cross alone is the answer to my need and yours. Only at the cross can you be pardoned. Only at the cross can a Holy God smile in forgiveness and love on guilty sinners like us. Because of this, Paul in rapture exclaimed, "God, forbid that I should glory, save in the cross of our Lord Jesus Christ!"

The cross is God's side of salvation. It was all God's doing. We had nothing whatsoever to do with it. It was the gracious act of a just and loving God to provide a righteous way of salvation for sinful and guilty humanity. Salvation is, first and foremost, the work of God—the operation of His own wisdom, love, and grace.

Chapter II

SALVATION—YOUR SIDE

If Christ died for us and paid for our sins, does it follow, then, that all men are automatically saved? Is there not something which we ourselves must do in order to be saved? If so, what is it? To put it in the words of one in the Scriptures, "What must I do to be saved?"

Every awakened soul raises this question, whether he knows the gospel or not. When any person comes to the place of longing for God's salvation and fellowship, the first question naturally is, "What must I do?" Many, unfortunately, are so obsessed with the idea that they are to do something that they become blinded to what God has already done for their salvation. Yet this question is logical and natural, in fact, inevitable. What must I do to be a Christian?

Men are not automatically saved on a wholesale basis simply by virtue of the fact that Christ died for them. There is a part which the individual must play. But let it be firmly fixed in your mind that the part we have left to play in salvation is a very simple and minor one. All that remains for us to do is to *accept by simple faith to our own account what Christ did for us on the cross.* All we need do is believe, accept, trust, and receive what Christ has done in our behalf.

Your part, then, in salvation is simple—FAITH. "By grace are ye saved," says God's Word, "through faith" (Eph. 2:8)

When the Philippian jailer cried out to Paul and Silas, "Sirs, what must I do to be saved?" the great apostle simply stated to that desperate, seeking soul, "Believe on the Lord Jesus Christ, and thou shalt be saved" (Acts 16:31). Yes, your side of salvation is just FAITH—simple, childlike, trusting faith. Nothing more is needed, nothing less will suffice, nothing else will do.

But another question will probably arise in your mind. Just what is faith? Faith seems to be hard for the human mind to grasp and harder yet to exercise. Yet it ought to be the simplest thing possible, and in a sense it is.

Faith embraces, first of all, knowledge, or understanding. This is true of any form of faith—even that exercised in a thousand ways in everyday life. You cannot believe something about which you know nothing. Faith comes in response to what we hear or learn. Whenever you hear about something, you either believe it or you do not believe it—you either exercise faith or you do not. Saving faith requires knowledge and understanding of the cross and of what Christ did there. When a soul hears the message that Christ died for his sins, saving faith is not born until that soul really grasps the fact that Christ, once and for all, completely answered for all of his sins, and there is nothing left to do but accept that to his own account.

Any soul who hears the gospel, that Christ died for his sins, and really grasps the glorious fact that salvation is now a finished work, wrought by Christ on our behalf, has the kernel of faith within him. Once that is comprehended, faith is well begun. I shall never forget the night when faith became mine. A man of God had dealt with me long and faithfully, pointing me to the cross and Christ's invitation to come and be saved, but it seemed that all I could see was my sin and unworthiness. He prayed, and I tried to, but I left the meeting that evening in spiritual darkness and misery. However, after reaching home, when I was on my knees beside my bed, the truth suddenly dawned upon my soul that Jesus Christ had actually paid the penalty for all my sins! They were answered for! They were expiated! They were atoned for! He died for me—for my sin! I understood for the first time the divine plan of salvation—faith was dawning. I knew now what Christ had done on the cross of calvary. Such knowledge is the first element of faith.

Faith also embraces decision. Once the glorious fact of the work on the cross is grasped, a decision is necessarily made— *to repent of sin and accept this Christ, or not.* There is this decision of faith that must be made, once the knowledge of salvation is grasped. There are people who have been brought up in Christian homes and have been recipients of gospel teaching all their lives; yet, notwithstanding this knowledge, they have never made that personal decision of accepting Christ.

The decision to accept Christ, of course, involves the decision to repent of sin, for everyone who understands a degree of spiritual truth knows that following Christ means forsaking sin. He who has not understood that is not yet enlightened unto faith. And it is this necessity of repentance from sin that keeps many from accepting Christ. The decision must be made. Having now understood what Christ did for me on the cross, and knowing that to accept and to follow Him means repentance and turning from my sins, I must decide which I will do. Alas, that some, knowing fully what is involved and understanding perfectly what salvation is and what accepting Christ consists of, decide to reject His grace and go on in their sinful way! Such have not exercised faith, for faith embraces decision. There must be not only the enlightenment of the mind but also the exercising of the will. Faith involves both the intellect and the will. Since Christ died for me, and I know that, the only thing that stands between me and salvation is my own will. What will my choice be as I gaze at Christ on the cross, paying for the guilt of my sin?

Consider an illustration or two. Suppose that you are ill, nigh unto death. Your relatives learn of a famous doctor who can treat such a disease as you have. He is called to your bedside. He diagnoses your case and prescribes the remedy. The medicine he prescribes is exceedingly expensive, but in spite of that fact, your relatives secure it, paying the enormous price at great sacrifice. Are you saved because the remedy has been prescribed and purchased and placed beside your bed? Of course not. You must take the remedy provided. If you refuse to do that, you will die. If you are willing to take the remedy, you live. Just so it is with salvation. You must accept what Christ has done for you, in order to be benefited by it.

Suppose that you want to make a trip to Europe by airplane. Your ticket is purchased and is in your hand. You look at the plane on the airport runway, declaring your knowledge of the craft and your confidence in it. Will that get you across the ocean? Certainly not. You must step on board. When the faith which you previously said you had in the craft thus goes into action and you actually board the ship, you will make the crossing—unless the ship fails. In the case of Christ, He, the Ship of Salvation, cannot fail. But have you exercised faith by stepping on board?

Have you made your decision? Have you accepted Christ, repenting of your sins and sincerely purposing in your heart to follow Him? If not, then this decision now faces you. What will you do with Jesus Christ? What will be your reaction to the fact that He died for you and now pleads with you to come to Him for full and free forgiveness? What is the answer of your will to this knowledge of the cross, which is now yours?

Blessed be the one who has made that decision! It is the decision of all decisions, for it determines your eternal destiny. If you have made it, if you have accepted Christ and repented of your sin, then your salvation is forever sealed.

To add another simple word, *faith is just believing the promises of God's Word.* The Word says, "As many as received him, to them gave he power to become the sons of God, even to them that believe on his name" (John 1:12). "Believe on the Lord Jesus Christ, and thou shalt be saved" (Acts 16:31). "Him that cometh to me (Christ's words) I will in no wise cast out" (John 6:37). "Come unto me, all ye that labour and are heavy laden, and I will give you rest" (Matt. 11:28—Christ's words also). "Whosoever believeth in him shall not perish, but have everlasting life" (John 3:16).

Will God keep His word? Will Christ fulfill His promises? Upon this depends our salvation—upon this alone hangs our faith. Hence, faith is, in the final and simplest analysis, believing the promises of God's Word, the Bible. If we do not cling to His promises, we can have no sure hope. But if His Word is sure, our salvation is secure.

Faith is a matter of clinging to the one and only hope of salvation, the Crucified Christ. You may not understand all the spiritual significances of the cross or all the theological explanations about the atonement, but you know that Christ did something there that answered for your sins, and you know that this alone is your hope of salvation. And to that crucified Saviour you cling in earnest, simple faith. Toplady expressed it beautifully when he wrote:

> Rock of ages, cleft for me,
>   Let me hide myself in thee;
> Let the water and the blood,
>   From thy riven side, which flowed,
> Be of sin the double cure,
>   Save from wrath and make me pure.

> Could my tears forever flow,
>   Could my zeal no languor know,
> These for sin could not atone;
>   Thou must save and Thou alone:
> In my hand no price I bring,
>   Simply to Thy cross I cling.

This last line well expresses what constitutes true, saving faith—"Simply to Thy cross I cling." A Christian who was having serious doubts concerning his salvation once confided his difficulties to me. He was in soul anguish. My counsel to him was that whenever those doubts recurred, he should simply say within his soul, "My one hope of salvation is Christ and His work on the cross; to Him will I cling for salvation, come what may; and if I go to hell, I will go there trusting Christ." I knew that no enlightened soul, as this man was, could think for one minute that he could go to hell trusting Christ. Try this method for yourself when you are tempted to doubt God's glorious salvation.

May we close this chapter with the words of another hymn—that of Charlotte Elliot?

Just as I am, without one plea,
  But that Thy blood was shed for me,
And that Thou bid'st me come to Thee,
  O Lamb of God! I come! I come!

Just as I am—Thou wilt receive,
  Wilt welcome, pardon, cleanse, relieve;
Because Thy promise I believe,
  O Lamb of God! I come! I come!

This is faith.

CHAPTER III

YOUR ASSURANCE OF SALVATION

Is assurance of salvation possible? Some religious people say that it is impossible for a person to know whether or not he actually possesses eternal life until he dies and stands before the judgment seat of God. They are quite surprised, sometimes even indignant, at the testimony of those Christians who say they have assurance that they are saved. There are indeed some true Christians who do not have the assurance of salvation and who think that such assurance in this life it is not possible to attain.

If being a Christian meant doing my best to follow Christ but never knowing at the end of each day whether I was one day nearer to heaven or to hell than I was the day before, Christianity would indeed be a rather lame affair. If Christ asked me to follow Him and to trust Him but in return gave me no assurance of my eternal destiny, then He would not be very much of a Saviour. A good many people have just such a conception of Christ and of Christianity.

But is this the Bible's picture? Does the New Testament picture the followers of Christ groping through life in darkness and uncertainty, never knowing until they die whether they are to be saved or lost? Is that the best God is offering us in Christ? Is that the best the Bible promises to us? Is that the best the Christian life can offer? Is that the best kind of a hope we can present to other people whom we ask to follow the Lord Jesus Christ? Is that the best message a preacher of the gospel can bring to hopeless men and women? Is that the best message the missionary can offer the heathen as he goes out to present Christ to them? Is the message of the gospel a message of doubt and uncertainty?

Assurance of salvation is possible! It is the believer's privilege to know that he has eternal life. The Apostle John says in his first epistle, "These things have I written unto you . . . that ye may know that ye have eternal life, and that ye may believe on the name of the Son of God" (I John 5:13). John wrote this entire epistle for the express purpose that the believers to whom he writes might know that they have eternal life. Actually, to deny the possibility of the believer's assurance of salvation would be to deny the message of the First Epistle of John, to say that it was written in vain; and that would be an insult to the Holy Spirit, who inspired John to write it. If some say that it is presumptuous for a Christian to know that he is saved, we reply in this way: Is it presumption to believe God? Is it not rather presumption to disbelieve God and to make Him a liar?

Christ promises eternal life as a present possession to all those who will put their trust in Him, and to doubt that you have eternal life after you have believed on Christ is actually to count Him untrue to His promises.

But how may an individual know that he has eternal life? These are three sources of this assurance: (1) the change that has been wrought in one's life; (2) the testimony of the Word of God; (3) the inward witness of the Holy Spirit.

The testimony of the Apostle Paul was, "If any man be in Christ, he is a new creature: old things are passed away; behold, all things are become new" (II Cor. 5:17). In the first place, when a soul comes to know Jesus Christ in real salvation, there is a divine transformation wrought in that life. The new nature of Christ is imparted to the soul, so that, as Scripture says, "We have become partakers of the divine nature." This new nature naturally gives rise to new affections in the soul, new likes, new dislikes, new loves and new hatreds. The things which the person once loved, he now hates. The things which he once hated, he now loves. The whole inward disposition of his life has been changed.

Not only is this change apparent to the inner consciousness of the individual himself, but his outward life also will appear different to those around him. The whole temper of his life will be changed. Often there is a complete change of disposition. There will be a change even in one's conversation as to topic and vocabulary.

After I was converted there were times of doubt regarding the genuineness of my salvation experience. But of one thing I was positively certain—there was a change within me. My whole outlook on life was different. I had a real desire to serve the Lord and to pray. I longed for fellowship with Him. I had a desire to learn His Word. I enjoyed being with Christian people. I loved the singing of gospel songs. I enjoyed going to meetings to hear the Word taught. All of this had been foreign to my nature before I became a Christian. Before, those things had little appeal for me, if any at all. Most remarkable of all was the change of vocabulary which came to me automatically upon my conversion. My language had been both foul and ungodly. I hardly knew how to express myself without using evil language. But after I let the Lord Jesus come into my heart, to my own surprise, that kind of language just faded away.

Furthermore, although I was young, I had been enslaved

to a number of evil habits. Among them was the tobacco habit, chewing as well as smoking. There was a craving in my system for it. But when I was converted, that craving disappeared. Although there was an occasional recurrence of the desire later, it was never strong enough to overcome me. I am not necessarily saying that because a person may be tempted to use tobacco, he is not a Christian; but the point I am making is that when one does meet the Lord, there will be changes within him, particularly in his desires.

If you can honestly say that a change has taken place in your life, altering your desires, affections, and inward nature from evil things to godliness, you may rest assured that such a change has been wrought by the Spirit of God, and it is a sign that you have been born of God. When a person becomes a Christian, he is "born again." Birth is the reception of life. The new birth is the reception of new life, spiritual life, the Christ life. The new birth and new life naturally means a new inner nature. If you are conscious of a new nature within, it is an evidence that you are born of God. Of course, the old nature is also there, and sometimes there is a conflict between the old and the new natures, but this very conflict is an evidence that you are a Christian.

Paul says, "The flesh lusteth against the Spirit, and the Spirit against the flesh: and these are contrary the one to the other: so that ye cannot do the things that ye would" (Gal. 5:17). If such a conflict is going on in you, it is a clear sign that a new life has been imparted to you and a new nature implanted within you. Your old nature, which is called the "flesh," wars against the nature of the "Spirit." So if you have accepted Christ as your Saviour, to the best of your knowledge, and if, as a result, you are conscious that a change has been wrought within you, this is an evidence that you are a real Christian—that you have been saved and made a child of God forever.

Secondly, the believer in the Lord Jesus Christ may have assurance of his salvation on the surest of all grounds—because God's Word asserts that he is a child of God. The testimony of the Bible is the testimony of God himself; therefore, whatever the Scriptures say is absolutely sure.

In John 1:12 we read: "As many as received him, to them gave he power (the right) to become the sons of God, even to them that believe on his name." Here is a clear statement in God's own Holy Word that everyone who receives Jesus and believes on Him for salvation positively becomes a child of God. In Acts 13:39 we read, "By him all that believe are justified from all things." To be justified means "to be declared just," to be declared free from the guilt of sin. Everyone who believes in Jesus may know that he is justified from all things, because the Word of God plainly so states. What better ground of assurance could one have than that?

The Lord Jesus Christ promised in John 5:24, "He that heareth my word, and believeth . . . hath everlasting life, and shall not come into condemnation; but is passed from death unto life." Now, certainly, if you have placed your faith in the Son of God as your Saviour, and if you are now trusting Him, then, on the basis of His own promise, you right now have eternal life and, on the basis of the same promise, will never come into judgment. Whether you "feel" saved or not, it is not feeling that matters, but what God's Word says. You can always trust God's Word, but you cannot always trust your feelings.

Many doubt their salvation and relationship to God merely on the ground of personal feeling, whereas they should accept assurance of their salvation on the ground of God's promises. The only question to ask is, have we met the conditions of these promises? That condition is FAITH in the finished work of Christ. If you are trusting in the finished work of Christ for your salvation, then God says that you are saved. What better ground of assurance could you have than the Word of God?

When Jesus said to the sinful woman in the house of Simon the Leper, "Thy sins are forgiven" (Luke 7:48), was it presumption for her to go out and say, "I know that all of my sins have been forgiven?" Would it not rather have been presumption for her to say that she doubted that her sins were forgiven? Is it any more presumptuous for a Christian today to say, "My sins are forgiven, and I know that I am saved," when God plainly states in His Word, "In whom (Christ) we have redemption through his blood, the forgiveness of sins, according to the riches of his grace" (Eph. 1:7)? Of the Ephesian Christians the Apostle Paul said, "God for Christ's sake hath forgiven you" (Eph. 4:32). The Apostle John says to the people whom he addresses in his epistle, "I write unto you, little children, because your sins are forgiven you for his name's sake" (I John 2:12). God's promise in the gospel is, "Whosoever shall call upon the name of the Lord shall be saved." If you have called upon the Lord Jesus Christ to save you, either He has saved you, or else God's promise does not stand.

In I John 5:11-12 we read: "This is the record, that God hath given us eternal life, and this life is in his Son. He that hath the Son hath life; and he that hath not the Son of God hath not life." Have you received the Lord Jesus Christ, God's Son into your heart? Have you asked Him to come into your life and to become your Saviour? Are you clinging to Him in that simple faith now? If so, then, on the basis of God's own Word, you have eternal life.

So if Satan should whisper doubts in your ears to the effect that your sins are not forgiven at all, point to the Word of God and say, "God says that my sins are forgiven, because I have believed in the Lord Jesus Christ, and I believe God." Then if Satan should lead you to think, "Well, perhaps I don't believe on Him," just say, "If I never did believe on Him before, I accept Him and believe on Him here and now." Then go on your way rejoicing, knowing that your sins are forgiven and that you are a child of God, on the basis of God's own written promises.

May we submit an illustration from Dr. R. A. Torrey? Suppose, says Torrey, that you were sentenced to imprisonment and that your friends secured a pardon for you. The legal document announcing your pardon is brought to you. You read it and know that you are pardoned, because the legal document says so, but the news is so good and so sudden that you are dazed by it. You do not realize that you are pardoned.

Someone comes to you and says, "Are you pardoned?"

What do you reply? You say, "Yes, I am pardoned."

Then he asks, "Do you feel pardoned?"

You reply, "No, I do not feel pardoned. It is so sudden, it is so wonderful, that I cannot realize it!"

Then he says to you, "But how can you know that you are pardoned, if you cannot feel it?"

You hold out the document and say, "This says so."

The time would come, after you had read the document again and again and had believed it, when you would not only know that you were pardoned, because the document says so, but you would feel it. Now the Bible is God's authoritative document declaring that everyone who believes in Jesus is justified, declaring that everyone who believes on the Son has everlasting life, declaring that everyone who receives Jesus is a child of God. If anyone asks you if your sins are all forgiven, just reply, "Yes, I know they are, because God says so." If someone asks you if you know that you are a child of God, reply, "Yes, I know that I'm a child of God, because He says so." If they ask you if you have eternal life, reply, "Yes, I know that I have eternal life, because God says so." You may not feel it yet, but if you will keep meditating upon God's statement and believing what God says, the time will come when you will feel it.

There is a third witness to the assurance of the believer's salvation—the Inward Presence and Voice of the Holy Spirit. The Bible says, "The Spirit itself beareth witness with our spirit, that we are the children of God" (Rom. 8:16). Actually, what some would call the "feeling" of salvation is not human feeling at all. It is the inward voice of God's Holy Spirit bearing witness to our spirits that we are children of God. It is not a human feeling but a divine impression. The Holy Spirit brings to our inner consciousness the vivid assurance that we are saved.

Of course, the Holy Spirit brings that assurance to us primarily through the Word of God itself. Yet often in heathen lands, where people are not even able to read and write, the Holy Spirit, in remarkable manners, has brought the blessed assurance of salvation even to ignorant and illiterate people. He was sent into our hearts to be our Comforter, and one of His main messages of comfort is the message of the assurance of our salvation. As a Christian reads the Word of God and meditates upon it with open heart, the Holy Spirit takes the truths of that Word and implants them firmly in the soul, bearing witness to the fact that he is Christ's.

This inward witness of the Holy Spirit is further strengthened and deepened as we commune with God in prayer. Prayer is not only petition, but it is also communion. Not only do we speak to God, but God, through His Holy Spirit, speaks back to us. So if you are troubled with doubts about your salvation, do not only search the Word of God, but go to Him in prayer. As you pray to God, the Holy Spirit will speak back to your heart and bring you the blessed assurance that you are His child. A Christian who doesn't pray is very apt to lose the assurance of his salvation, because it is as we pray that the Holy Spirit communicates to us that assurance.

When your heart becomes heavy and the wheels of your chariot drag, so to speak, go to the Lord in prayer and let the Holy Spirit comfort your heart by His voice of assurance and hope. The very fact that you find comfort and assurance as you pray is, in itself, an evidence that you are a child of God, because only to such does the Holy Spirit communicate.

Do not think that you have to go through life wondering whether you are saved or lost. The change in your own heart and life, the testimony of God's Word, and the inward witness of the Holy Spirit all unite to bring to the true Christian a definite assurance that he is saved for time and eternity. When doubts persist, look back again to the Christ of the cross and say, "He died for my sins. He paid my penalty. He promised that if I would trust Him as my Substitute, He would save me. I have trusted Him. Now I depend on Him to keep His promise."

Some new converts make the mistake of falling into despondency and feeling that they are lost, when the fervency of their first love for Christ seems to wane. Bear in mind that our human frames and feelings and affections may change with the state of our health, the state of the weather, the cir-

cumstances in which we find ourselves, and through many
other causes; but Jesus Christ never changes! He is the same
yesterday, today, and forever.

Robert Boyd has said, "We have known some who never
thought that they had any enjoyment of religion unless they
were in the midst of high excitement. The meeting that did
not melt them into tears or lift them into the heights of ec-
static rapture was not a good meeting. The calm statement of
divine truth, the earnest study of the Bible to know the will
of God, the prayerfulness and self-examination of the closet,
all appear to such persons as dull and uninteresting. They are
like a habitual reader of exciting and sensational novels; they
have no relish for what is solid and instructive." My dear
reader, avoid this at the very beginning of your Christian
career, and let Jesus, who alone is the author, be also the
finisher of your faith.

CHAPTER IV

YOUR FELLOWSHIP WITH GOD

Now that you have become a child of God, the greatest privilege in the world for a human being is possible to you—namely, fellowship with Almighty God. Fellowship with God! The very expression almost overcomes one with awe and wonder. How is fellowship with God possible for a sinful being? It is possible purely on the grounds of the CROSS. At the cross a holy God and a sinful man can meet on common ground, because it was there that He dealt with our sin. There God can and will meet us.

In the Old Testament Moses was instructed to erect a tabernacle in which God would dwell. In that tabernacle he was to build a "holiest" place, and in that holiest place he was to set what was called "the mercy seat." The mercy seat was made of pure gold, and once each year the blood of atonement was sprinkled upon it. Concerning that blood-sprinkled mercy seat, God said to His people of old, "There will I meet thee." God could meet the nation of Israel in the person of their high priest there at the mercy seat, because the blood of atonement which He promised to accept had been sprinkled on it in their behalf. It was the blood of atonement that cleared the ground for a meeting between a holy God and sinful man. Just so it is with the blood of the cross. At the cross God will meet any soul who will place his trust in the blood that was shed there as an atonement for his sins.

Hence, fellowship with God is possible because of the cross and because of our faith in the work of the cross. In the New Testament we read, "Having therefore, brethren, boldness to enter into the holiest by the blood of Jesus, by a new and living way . . . and having an high priest over the house of God; let us draw near with a true heart in full assurance of faith" (Heb. 10:19-22). In another place in the same epistle we read, "Seeing then that we have a great high priest, that is passed into the heavens, Jesus the Son of God . . . Let us therefore come boldly unto the throne of grace, that we may obtain mercy, and find grace to help in time of need" (Heb. 4:14-16).

It is on the ground, then, of the cross and our faith in the cross that we are able to have fellowship with God.

How is this fellowship with God cultivated? This celestial fellowship is cultivated by the habitual practice of prayer and by ever living in an atmosphere of prayer. It may sound almost axiomatic, but fellowship is cultivated by fellowship. As you visit with a person and spend time with him, your fellowship with him deepens, and your acquaintance becomes more fixed. The more time you spend together, the richer the fellowship becomes. It is precisely the same way with our fellowship with God. As far as God is concerned, the way is cleared on His side for fellowship for all those who trust the finished work of Christ on the cross. Let us beware that nothing within us hinders us on our side from having fellowship with Him.

Not only is this fellowship with God cultivated through prayer, but also through the reading of God's Word. When we pray, we are talking to God. When we read the Word, God is talking to us. Thus, our fellowship with God is cultivated when we spend time praying and searching His Word.

We shall say more about the Bible later.

How is this fellowship with God maintained? Sometimes sin on our part breaks that fellowship, and we do not enjoy the presence of God. Fellowship is maintained by our purposing in our hearts to walk separate from sin and by confessing and forsaking sin just as soon as we become conscious of it. Unconfessed sin always breaks fellowship with God. But as soon as confession is made, and God sees in us a heart broken and contrite over the sin and failure, the fellowship is restored. David cried out, "A broken and a contrite heart, O God, thou wilt not despise!" Before writing this, David had been guilty of a very grievous combination of sins, and his fellowship with God had been so completely broken that he cried out to God, "Cast me not away from thy presence; and take not thy holy spirit from me. Restore unto me the joy of thy salvation; and uphold me with thy free spirit." When God saw his contrition of heart and heard his confession of sin, He immediately restored David to His fellowship.

Naturally, no one can maintain fellowship with God while walking in sin. Though a Christian may fall into sin and even continue in it for a time, he cannot maintain fellowship with God in so doing. Fellowship with God is maintained by a continual confession of every conscious sin—and not only confession of sin, but the forsaking of all known sin. So, Christian, when you realize that you have sinned against God, go to Him immediately, make confession, and plead His forgiveness and restoration. He will be true to His Word and restore you again to fellowship with Himself.

This fellowship with God in the Christian life is really something that is indispensable. Without such fellowship the Christian does not experience the true joy of the Lord.

The Lord intends His people to have joy. Christ said to his disciples, "These things have I spoken unto you, that my joy might remain in you, and that your joy might be full" (John 15:11). Peter says, "Whom having not seen, ye love; in whom, though now ye see him not, yet believing, ye rejoice with joy unspeakable and full of glory" (I Pet. 1:8). The Apostle Paul wrote to the Philippian Christians, "Rejoice in the Lord alway: and again I say, Rejoice" (Phil. 4:4). In another place he stated, "For the kingdom of God is not meat and drink; but righteousness, and peace, and joy in the Holy Ghost" (Rom. 14:17).

All through the Bible there is much emphasis on the fact that God wants His saved people to be happy and joyful. But when one does not walk in fellowship with God, one loses the joy of salvation. Happy Christians are those who live in close fellowship with God—those who pray and read God's Word. The joy of matrimony consists in fellowship between husband and wife. When that happy fellowship is broken, the joy of marriage is gone. The joy of a home consists of happy fellowship between all the members of the family. When that fellowship is broken, the joy of the home is destroyed.

Fellowship with God is indispensable to a life of victory over sin and Satan. Prayer, the reading of God's Word, and vital fellowship with God are sources of spiritual strength. The Christian who backslides began his backsliding by neglecting this matter of cultivating fellowship with God. If you fail to live in fellowship with God, praying and reading God's Word, you will begin to drift away from the Lord. It will not be long until you fall into sin, and Satan will have victory over you. Satan is too strong for us to meet him in our own strength. We have to derive strength from the Lord, and that strength is appropriated as we fellowship with Him daily. No Christian can be strong spiritually and triumph over sin and the world if he does not live a life of prayer and fellowship with the Lord. Satan knows that full well, and that is the reason he tries so hard to keep us from praying. Satan would rather have us do anything else in the world than pray.

Fellowship with God is also indispensable to bearing fruit for the Lord. In the fifteenth chapter of John's Gospel, Jesus illustrated the relationship between Himself and the Christian by the union of the vine and the branch. He pointed out that the branch can bear fruit only as it abides in the vine and draws its life and fruit-bearing qualities from the vine. Then the Saviour says, "Abide in me, and I in you. As the branch cannot bear fruit of itself, except it abide in the vine; no more can ye, except ye abide in me . . . for without me ye can do nothing." A branch that does not live by its union with the vine and by drawing its sap from the vine will soon be dead and useless. Likewise it is with us as Christians. If we fail to abide in Christ, to live in constant, conscious fellowship with Him, our lives will become dead and barren. Only as we live and abide in fellowship with our Saviour can we bring forth fruit. If you are teaching a Sunday school class, if you are the leader of a young people's group, if you are trying to win souls by personal contact, bear in mind that apart from fellowshipping with Christ constantly, deriving the inner strength from Him which is needed for the task, you will accomplish little or nothing.

A saintly Christian has said, "If you keep a constant nearness to Christ, taking Him as your only hope and His spotless life as your bright example, there will be seen in your life a spiritual progress, brighter and brighter, to the perfect day. With knowledge in your mind, grace in your heart, and obedience in your life, there will be such a symmetry of character as will lead men to glorify your father in heaven. In the hard conflict with your besetting sins Christ will be your strength; nor will He leave you till your last foe lies vanquished on the field. Rash and impetuous passions will be displaced by calm and holy repose in God. Unholy bursts of imperious temper will be subdued by the meekness of Jesus. Peevish impatience will give way to holy submission to God's will. Worldly-mindedness will be overcome by communion with God and a clearer conception of the grandeur and glory of eternal things."

Someone else has said, "Instead of making your religion bend to your worldly convenience, make your worldly convenience bend to your religion. Pray earnestly and believingly for growth in grace and for strength to support you amid the trials and temptations of life; but do not put prayer in the place of duties which you yourself ought to do."

While we must beware of dead formalism in our prayer life, a few simple rules and purposes of heart will be helpful —yes, indispensable. *First of all,* begin the day with God in thanksgiving and prayer. As you think of the new blessings which God gives you each day, give thanks to Him for them. Then as you think of the temptations that you may meet during the day, ask God to give you strength for victory over them. Anticipate your battles on your knees in the morning, and claim His overcoming grace. Never let the rush of the day's business cheat you out of your morning watch with the Lord.

Second, stop in the midst of the hustle and bustle of the day from time to time for thanksgiving and prayer. A few moments alone with God off and on throughout the day will keep you calm and triumphant in the midst of life's cares and turmoils.

Third, close the day with thanksgiving and prayer. When you come to the end of the day, before you retire, review the blessings of the day and thank God for them in detail.

Fourth, the last thing to do each day is to ask God to forgive all the things in your life that you know have been displeasing to Him that day. Confess your sin honestly before Him for both forgiveness and cleansing. Pause for a moment during your prayer and let the Holy Spirit search your heart, to point out any sins of which you may not be conscious.

Remember the motto that you see in so many places, which is no less true because it is so common: "Prayer changes things." Prayer is your source of victory. Prayer is your source of fruitfulness. Prayer is primarily communion with God. Fellowship with God is not only a privilege, but it is an indispensable factor in a successful Christian life.

CHAPTER V

YOUR FELLOWSHIP WITH GOD'S PEOPLE

The company a person keeps has a great deal to do with the character he produces. One's spiritual life, as well as his intellectual and social life, is helped or hindered by the companionship he habitually chooses. It is important, therefore, for every Christian to choose spiritual friends for his intimate companions and to deliberately cultivate Christian fellowship.

In the Book of Proverbs, which is the most practical and homely book of the Old Testament, there is much said about friends and companions. Let us quote a few of these statements: "He that walketh with wise men shall be wise: but a companion of fools shall be destroyed" (13:20); "A poor man is better than a liar" (19:22); "Make no friendship with an angry man; and with a furious man thou shalt not go: Lest thou learn his ways, and get a snare to thy soul" (22: 24, 25); "Confidence in an unfaithful man in time of trouble is like a broken tooth, and a foot out of joint" (25:19).

No matter who we are or how strong our character and Christian life may be, we are all affected by the company we keep. And since we are social beings, requiring social fellowship and companionships, let us, as Christians, choose, cherish, and cultivate real Christian friends.

For your most intimate associates select a few friends of about your own age who have an interest in the study of the

Bible, in prayer, and in winning others to Christ. On the other hand, avoid close companionship with those who you know are spiritually and morally hurtful to you. A Christian need not utterly withdraw himself from unconverted people, but he should avoid making them his intimate friends. If you find, in spite of all your efforts, that your companionship is doing harm to your spiritual life, then give it up.

Now do not get the idea that the Christian life is a lonely one, devoid of all good fellowship and social relations. Not at all! The richest friendship in all the world is found among Christians. It was the social oneness and harmony among the Christians of the first centuries that impressed the heathen rulers with Christianity and caused the Roman Emperor Constantine to espouse the Christian faith and proclaim it as the official religion of his empire. The heathen people in whose midst those early Christians lived could not comprehend their love and devotion to each other and the pure fellowship that existed among them.

In Christ social and class hatreds and prejudices are swept away, and men and women become conscious of their oneness in Him. On mission fields I have seen members of tribes and races that had actually hated each other like dogs and snakes, work, live, and pray together like blood brothers. I have seen embittered Jews and arrogant Arabs in North Africa, made one in Christ, enjoying the holiest of fellowship around the Lord's Table as well as in daily life. I have known people in our own country who have hated each other for years to become the most intimate of fellows after conversion.

Christian fellowship even transcends the barriers of human language. One time an American Christian in London, England, met a European Christian in one of the city parks. Both were away from their homes in a city of strangers, and, there-

fore, both were feeling somewhat lonely. As one looked at
the other in the park, each somehow understood that the other
was a Christian, and this mutual understanding drew them
together. When they met, one of them exclaimed, "Hallelu-
jah!" and the other responded with a resounding, "Amen!"
With only these two words, both were uplifted and blessed
by their contact and fellowship. There is a common tie that
binds Christian hearts together and a common language that
transcends linguistic vocabularies.

> Blest be the tie that binds
>   Our hearts in Christian love;
> The fellowship of kindred minds
>   Is like to that above.
>
> Before our Father's throne,
>   We pour our ardent prayers;
> Our fears, our hopes, our aims are one,
>   Our comforts and our cares.
>
> We share our mutual woes,
>   Our mutual burdens bear;
> And often for each other flows
>   The sympathizing tear.

T. J. Bach, well-known missionary and Christian leader for
the past half-century, very aptly defined "fellowship" as "two
fellows in the same ship." Two fellows in the same ship, out
on the ocean's billows, away from everything else, are going to
have a lot in common. They must work the ship together,
they must weather the storm together, and they must share
their provisions. A breach between them would be tragic,
to say the very least. It might even be disastrous.

Satan is exceedingly busy in our generation, trying to disrupt the fellowship of Christians. He tries to do this between churches, denominations, and groups—even where they are united in acceptance of the cardinal truths of the Christian faith. He tries it within the churches, among the ranks of the members. He tries it between Christian leaders, even the great stalwarts of the church. He tries it between Christian workers. He tries it between Christian neighbors. He tries it in the Christian family—in the home. He tries it between Christian friends. He tries everywhere and all the time to jar and mar the fellowship of Christians.

Disrupted fellowship among God's people is a tragedy. Our Saviour is grieved by it, for He prayed that His followers "all may be one; as thou, Father, art in me, and I in thee, that they also may be one in us: that the world may believe" (John 17:21). The Holy Spirit is grieved by it, for by Him we have all been baptized into one body (I Cor. 12:13). In Ephesians 4:30-32 we read: "And grieve not the holy Spirit of God, whereby ye are sealed unto the day of redemption. Let all bitterness, and wrath, and anger, and clamour, and evil speaking, be put away from you, with all malice: and be ye kind one to another, tenderhearted, forgiving one another, even as God for Christ's sake hath forgiven you." The Christian himself loses the joy of the Lord by disrupted fellowship with God's other children. Prayer is hindered. Testimony is weakened. Spiritual power is lost. Unsaved people are perplexed. Our children are confused and sometimes led astray. So Satan's havoc takes a sweeping toll both on earth and in heaven.

Christian fellowship needs to be cultivated, and it needs to be guarded. Christian, definitely cultivate fellowship with other Christians. Go regularly to some good church, so that you can really cultivate intimate fellowship with the people.

If you go constantly from one place to another, it is hard to establish such fellowship. Invite Christians into your home for informal social companionship. Arrange picnics and other wholesome outings with Christian families. Ask them to pray for you and your problems; in turn, pray for theirs, and tell them so. Pray together with them in informal prayer get-togethers.

One excellent plan is to find a "prayer partner." Select someone of approximately your own age, and then share your prayer burdens. Try to get together once a week at a fixed time to pray over these problems—just the two of you. Of course, in cultivating fellowship with other Christians it is to be understood that there must be the social side to that fellowship as well as the spiritual. You will not necessarily always be praying or talking about spiritual things. The purely "human" side of your nature, as well as the spiritual side, must be fed by fellowship with others. Christian fellowship should be versatile and universal. It should include eating together, playing together, helping one another in material things, traveling together, and just visiting or chatting.

Remember that the responsibility of cultivating such fellowship is yours as much as the other person's. "He that hath friends (or wishes to have friends) must shew himself friendly" (Prov. 18:24). And when you have made friends, prize and guard their friendships. Do not be selfish and peevish. Overlook small faults. We all have them. Do not betray confidences. Do not let out of your mouth all that has entered your ears. Listen to the counsel of the wisest man on earth on this matter of fellowship: "A friend loveth at all times" (Prov. 17:17). "He that covereth a transgression seeketh love; but he that repeateth a matter separateth very friends" (Prov. 17.9). "The words of a talebearer are as wounds" (Prov.

18:8). "A brother offended is harder to be won than a strong city" (Prov. 18:19). "A talebearer revealeth secrets: but he that is of a faithful spirit concealeth the matter" (11:13).

Solomon also warned against overdoing fellowship, against getting "too thick," as we say in modern slang. "Withdraw thy foot from thy neighbor's house; lest he be weary of thee, and so hate thee" (25:17). This warning is particularly wise where children are involved. When anything occurs to strain the fellowship between you and your Christian friends, go to them quickly and frankly and get the fog cleared away. Where you have been at fault, confess. Where they have been at fault, forgive. Above all, forget the matter completely, and let the fellowship continue. Christian friends are too valuable to lose and too hard to replace; they are, in fact, indispensable to your spiritual walk.

If, to become a follower of Jesus Christ, it was necessary for you to give up some, or, perhaps, even the majority of your old friends, do not be alarmed, for you will have better friends in Christ than you ever had in the world. That surely was my experience. And this is Christ's very promise (Matt. 19:29). You will find that your Christian friends are your real friends, despite some exceptions, of course, which we must be prepared to face, for there are always hypocrites as well as true men and women of God.

I have found Christian friends who have stood with me in the gaps, through thick and thin, where worldly friends would have fled and forgotten me. The wordling is, after all, a selfish person. The Christian has the love of God and the compassion of Christ in his heart. A self-centered man will think of himself, but a Christ-centered man will think of others. Actually, those people who stand between you and God and keep you away from the Lord Jesus Christ are not really your friends, after all. They are your worst enemies. Any man who will keep another man from serving God is that man's foe, not his friend.

So if you want friends, true friends, friends who will help you in every way, seek Christian friends. If you want to succeed and grow in your Christian life, seek Christian fellowship. If you want your life to glow and tell most for Christ, cultivate real Christian companionship. You may fall if you walk alone. But if you walk in company with other saints, there will always be someone to support and strengthen you.

One Saturday evening, a few years ago, I was very discouraged. I met a Christian with whom I was quite intimate, and we spent the evening together, chatting, visiting, and praying. I said nothing to him about my discouragement. When we parted, close to the midnight hour, I was so lifted up in spirit that I almost felt like going out and looking for some more trouble! A couple of weeks later we met again. About the first thing that my friend said to me was, "You know, I was so discouraged when we met that night that I almost felt like giving up. But after we spent that evening together, my faith and courage were renewed and revived. I was lifted up. I wanted to tell you about it." Here is a perfect example of the value of Christian fellowship. Two discouraged Christians spent a few hours of fellowship together, and both were lifted out of their gloom! Cultivate a few true, intimate Christian friends. When you are discouraged or in trouble, seek their fellowship.

Christian fellowship is one of the sweetest, most wholesome and most uplifting things there is on this side of heaven.

CHAPTER VI

YOUR SPIRITUAL DIET

Spiritual life is likened in the Word of God to our natural, physical life, and it must be similarly sustained by correct and careful nourishment. The new life was imparted to us in a *new birth* when we accepted the Saviour. If a newborn babe should be left without proper care and nourishment, could he be expected to grow and develop? Likewise, the spiritual life, i.e., the Christian life, must be properly nurtured and nourished if it is to prosper and grow. *Becoming* a Christian is a matter of birth (the new birth); *being* a Christian is a matter of growth. "Grow in grace," Peter exhorts, "and in the knowledge of our Lord and Saviour Jesus Christ" (II Pet. 3:18).

All life is dependent upon food for growth. So God, in His wisdom and grace, has provided richly for the feeding and care of our spiritual life. That provision is His Word, the Holy Bible. It contains a balanced diet for the soul, providing every spiritual vitamin needed for health and growth. It provides pure milk, sweet honey, living bread, the water of life, strong meat, and all manner of rich fruits. (All of these similies are used in the Bible itself concerning its own contents.)

The Christian who will feed his soul daily or several times daily with the Word of God, as he does his body with physical food, will be a strong, healthy child of God. You can be a giant spiritually instead of a weakling. But without this daily diet, no Christian can be strong.

Read your Bible. Read it diligently, earnestly seeking to grasp its truths and assimilate its blessings. Careless reading of it will not help much. If the average person would read his school textbooks as carelessly and indifferently as he does the Bible, he would not get far in his education. On the other hand, if the average person would read the Bible with as much diligence as he does his ordinary textbooks, he would find the majority of it to be understandable to him. People often complain that they cannot understand the Bible, when perhaps they have not really tried. If any Christian will undertake to read carefully through the New Testament, beginning with the first chapter of Matthew, he will probably be amazed at how understandable the Bible really is to him. And as he reads and absorbs its truths, his spiritual life will be strangely fed and nurtured. Approach the Bible with the intention and purpose of understanding it, and understand it you will.

One of the modern English versions now available will greatly aid a new reader in understanding the Bible. There are several excellent ones of the New Testament in particular. A favorite among Bible readers for a number of years has been the Weymouth Translation. The Berkeley Version is very good, as is the Centenary Translation. A recent good one is the Williams Translation, published by the Moody Press. We recommend that you secure at least one of these versions.

Read your Bible regularly and systematically. Sporadic and haphazard reading of it will neither satisfy nor suffice. A regular time should be set apart each day for Bible reading. Reading in connection with your prayer time is best—possibly preceding your prayer. Not less than fifteen minutes of Bible reading daily, at the very lowest minimum, can suffice to sustain any Christian's spiritual life. Two fifteen-minute periods each day ought to be our minimum goal. Many saints of God spend an hour a day in studying the Bible.

No matter how busy you think you are, do not be too busy to feed your soul. It is a tragedy when a man becomes so busy making a living that he cannot take time to eat. Of course, that does not often happen; but frequently we meet Christians who are so busy making a physical living that they starve their Christian lives to nothingness. Is that not a tragedy? If you want to be a real Christian, be a Bible Christian— read God's Word regularly.

In prayer we talk to God. In the Bible God talks to us. The two go together. Dr. Torrey has said, "Any day that is allowed to pass without faithful Bible study is a day thrown open to the advent into our hearts and lives of error or sin." It is at this very point that many begin to fail and then later fall.

Read your Bible obediently. Nothing actually brings one nearer to an understanding of the Bible than the purpose to obey it. No one can appreciably understand the Scriptures without a willingness to obey its injunctions. This is without doubt frequently the cause of failure to understand it. The Lord Jesus said, "If any man willeth to do His will, he shall know of the teaching" (John 7:17, R.V.). It is amazing how quickly one begins to lose his relish for Bible reading and how soon the mind fails to get hold of its teachings, when there has been open disobedience to any of its commands. To obey its truths when they are seen prepares one to see other truths. To disobey a recognized truth is to darken your mind and heart to all of its truths. Many have sadly proved this by their experience. Cultivate prompt, complete, happy, unquestioning obedience to every command in the Book that clearly applies to you, and you will find that every command is a signboard to mark the way to further truths and richer blessings.

A friend of mine who has left a deep mark for good on my own life once said in my hearing, "Years ago I made up my mind that as I read the Bible, I would, by God's grace, attempt to do everything it commanded me." That remark at once explained to me his Christlikeness and spiritual power. He has let the word of God accomplish its purpose in him.

Read your Bible prayerfully, asking the Spirit of God to reveal its truths to you and to apply them to your life. The Bible is God's inspired Word, and it cannot be understood with merely the natural mind. Those who read it so will never arrive at a real knowledge of its contents. But those who pray, like David, as they search it, "Open thou mine eyes, that I may behold wondrous things out of thy law," will find its truths ever unfolding to them as they read and meditate. First Corinthians 2:12 tells us: "Now we have received, not the spirit of the world, but the Spirit which is of God; that we might know the things that are freely given to us of God . . . not in the words which man's wisdom teacheth, but which the Holy Ghost teacheth . . . but the natural man receiveth not the things of the Spirit of God: for they are foolishness unto him: neither can he know them, because they are (to be) spiritually discerned. But he that is spiritual judgeth all things." Only those who are divinely enlightened can grasp spiritual truth. And the Bible is, of course, primarily a Book of spiritual truth.

Every time you open its pages, though it be for only a few minutes, ask the Spirit of God to give you the power to discern and grasp the meaning. And whenever you encounter a diffi-

culty in the Scriptures, lay it before the Lord and ask Him to
give you the explanation. Jesus gave the promise, "When
He the Spirit of Truth is come, He shall guide you into all
the truth" (John 16:13, R.V.). He is the real Author of the
Bible and its best Teacher and Interpreter. He will serve
you thus when you ask Him.

Commentaries on the Bible definitely have their value, but
one will learn more of the deeper spiritual truths of its pages
through the direct aid of the Holy Sprit than from all the
books ever written about it. Even the most humble believer
in Christ, who might not be able to make use of the scholarly
commentaries, is given the privilege of having the assistance of the Spirit and, hence, an understanding of the Scriptures. So read the Bible ever with a prayer on your lips and
a heart open to the blessed Spirit of God. If the Bible is read
with only the natural understanding, its deepest truths will
never be grasped, and the result may only be confusion and
difficulty.

Read your Bible incessantly. Carry a small New Testament
on your person all the time, or even a pocket edition of the
whole Bible, and read it during those few-minute periods in
every person's life which are usually lost. While riding on
streetcars or trains, while waiting for meals, while relaxing
from work, any time you find a few spare minutes, read the
Word of God. Such little snatches of feasting will be to your
spiritual life what a snack or tidbit is to your physical system
during the day. Never be without at least a portion of
the Scriptures, and use every golden moment you can find to
feed upon it. In that way you will become a robust Christian
and not remain a babe.

Memorize your Bible. David long ago declared, "Thy word
have I hid in mine heart, that I might not sin against thee" (Ps.

119:11). The Revised Version of this verse says, "Thy Word have I laid up in my heart." There is great value in memorizing the Word of God. First of all, as David states, the Word learned by heart and, thus, ever fresh before the mind restrains us from sinning. During the moment of the temptation a verse previously committed to memory will flash into the mind and hold us back from committing the sinful act. It serves as a restraining force, and a very powerful one, too. To know this in reality, one must experience it. Will you not put this to the test?

Scripture committed to memory also equips one to be a soul-winner and a witness to others. God always honors and uses His Word; on the other hand, He cannot always do so with our own words and arguments. When human urging and reasoning fall dull and flat on people's minds, the Word of God remains "quick (living), and powerful, and sharper than any twoedged sword . . . and is a discerner of the thoughts and intents of the heart" (Heb. 4:12). He who attempts witnessing and soul-winning without having God's Word ready on his lips will be put to great disadvantage. Especially do we need the "thus saith the Lord" on our tongues when we desire to exhort or rebuke a fellow Christian who may be in need of such. When your reasoning and persuading will be empty and void, statements from the divine Word will convince, convict, and sanctify.

There are various practical ways and aids for Scripture memorization. A simple suggestion for every day is to memorize one verse selected from your regular Bible reading—perhaps the verse that has meant the most to you on that day. Underline it in your Bible or Testament and review it at various times during the day in that inevitable spare minute or two. Also keep reviewing those previously learned. Constant repetition is the secret of memorization. (If one verse per day seems beyond your time and ability, do not be discouraged; start out with one a week instead.) A good method for helping to keep memorized verses fresh in the mind is to type them on little cards like calling cards and carry them with you in a small packet, so that you may run over them repeatedly during idle moments.

There is an organization in America for the express purpose of aiding people in Scripture memorization. It is called "The Navigators." The address is Colorado Springs, Colorado. This organization was begun among servicemen before World War II, and it has helped thousands to learn the Word of God from memory. Hundreds of personal soul-winners all over the country are the fruit of this fine work. Write to the Navigators for information regarding their card method of memorizing the Word of God, for it is the most helpful method we can recommend. They will supply you with selected verses already printed on cards in a little packet entitled "Beginning With Christ."

CHAPTER VII

YOUR SPIRITUAL DIET (Cont.)

Study your Bible. In addition to the daily reading of the Scriptures for personal devotional and inspirational purposes, every person who wants to succeed in being a real Christian must earnestly study the Bible. To find time for this is, we know, a real problem, but every true Christian will be able to set aside some time at regular periods for the purpose. "There is nothing more important for the development of the spiritual life of the Christian than regular, systematic Bible study" (Torrey). What the minister gives in his weekly sermons does not of itself suffice. You must study God's Word for yourself. One cannot depend on others to gather all of one's spiritual manna. Each must gather for himself.

Many Christians are confused, and not a few are misled by the various false religious cults and doctrines that have sprung up in our day. There are many of these, and they are on the increase. The only remedy against the snare of these false religions is a thorough knowledge of the truths of the Bible, gained by personal study in a firsthand way. Read Paul's farewell words to the elders of Ephesus, as recorded in Acts 20:29-32. Our spiritual health, our growth, our strength, our victory over sin, our soundness in doctrine, our joy and peace in Christ, our cleansing from inward and outward sin, our fitness for service—all depend upon the study of the Word of God. The one who fails to study his Bible will likely fail in Christian living, but he who really studies his Bible will succeed in living a real Christian life.

One method of Bible study is *the chapter method*. Select a certain book of the Bible and read it through, chapter by chapter, spending as much time as is required to master the contents of each chapter. Here again we wish to quote from Dr. R. A. Torrey, who says, "Read each chapter through several times and then answer the following questions:

"1. What is the principal subject of the chapter? (State the principal contents in a single phrase or sentence.)

"2. What is the truth most clearly taught and most emphasized in the chapter?

"3. What is the best lesson?

"4. What is the best verse?

"5. Who are the principal people mentioned?

"6. What does the chapter teach about Jesus Christ?

"7. What new truth have you learned from the chapter?

"8. What definite thing have you resolved to do as a result of studying this chapter?"

Go through book after book of the Book in this way, and you will be its master.

Another method of studying the Bible is *the topical method.* This was the chief method the famous preacher D. L. Moody used when he studied the Scriptures. It is a very simple and valuable method. To pursue it requires a few helps, but they are easily obtainable. You will need a topical textbook and (or) a good concordance, such as Cruden's. *The New Chain Reference Bible,* published by B. B. Kirkbride Bible Company, and the *Indexed Bible,* published by the Dickson Company, contain excellent helps along this line. (Any of these helps can be secured by contacting your nearest religious book store or by consulting your pastor.) Even the marginal references of an ordinary Bible will be of great assistance in this method of study.

Take your topical textbook or concordance and study all of the Bible verses you can find on such topics as the Holy Spirit, sin, grace, the blood of Christ, justification, faith, repentance, the new birth, the resurrection (of Christ, of believers, of all), the love of God, our love (to God, to Christians, to all men), the coming of Christ, heaven, hell, and other important truths. With the aids you are using, go through the entire Bible on each of the topics you may be studying.

A topical book (*The New Topical Textbook* is best), as well as the other helps mentioned, will be a great aid to those who desire to prepare Bible talks or lessons for use in services and classes. It is a wonderful method for giving devotional talks. By it one can virtually make an exhaustive study of any Bible doctrine or theme and always have a "thus saith the Lord" upon which to stand.

The book method is another good means of Bible study. (This is otherwise called the synthetic method). Dr. James M. Gray, long-time president of the Moody Bible Institute, was the leading advocate of this plan. We recommend that you secure his little book called "How to Master the English Bible," which explains it. This can be ordered from the Moody Press, Chicago. The plan is to pick out a certain book of the Bible, preferably one of the shorter New Testament epistles, to begin with, and master its contents by reading the entire book through numerous times, each time at one sitting, or even several times at a sitting. After about the second reading, begin to look for the main teaching of that book. At the next reading begin to note how the theme is developed. Then in subsequent readings make an outline of your own on it, bearing in mind that main, central theme.

Stay in one book until you feel that you have mastered it. Then go on to another. Within the course of your Christian life you may master the entire Bible. *It can be done*—it is, in fact, not as difficult as you may now think.

The character method is also a helpful method of studying the Bible. Here again your topical textbook, or one of the special Bibles referred to above, will be invaluable. This method is simply to choose some Bible character and study exhaustively all that the Bible says about him. Take such characters as Noah, Abraham, Lot, Jacob, Joseph, Moses, Joshua, Gideon, Samson, Samuel, Saul, David, Solomon, Isaiah, Jonah, John the Baptist, Peter, Thomas, Paul, Timothy. Compile a list of facts about the character being studied, such as:

1. His meeting with God, or conversion
2. His call to service
3. His strong points (such as faith, prayer, etc.)
4. His weak points (sins, failures)
5. His accomplishments
6. His influence
7. His name (note changes in names of some men—look up the meaning of their names)
8. What you should follow in his life
9. What you should avoid in his life
10. What God said about him

Study the Bible by *the comparative method*. By this we simply mean comparing Scripture with Scripture. The best commentary on the Bible is the Bible itself. When you are studying a certain portion or chapter of the Bible and you find a difficult passage which you do not understand, try to find another passage similar to it, or at least one dealing with the same subject, and let that explain its meaning. The best help for this method, in addition to the marginal references, which are often inadequate, is a book called *The Treasury of Scripture Knowledge,* which gives a large number of other references to every single verse of the Bible. A great Bible teacher said, "One will get more light on passages of Scripture by looking up the references given in *The Treasury of Scripture Knowledge* than in any other way I know."

There are some very fine courses of Bible study already prepared that can easily be secured at a very slight cost. One of these is the "Through the Bible Studies," prepared by Dr. Harlin Roper, of Dallas, Texas. These lessons consist of questions asked on each successive chapter of the Bible, the object being for the student to find the answers to these questions in the chapter and to write them in the space provided in the booklet. A series of several small, inexpensive booklets cover the entire Bible, and they form an excellent method of Bible study. For samples and information, write to the "Through the Bible" Publishers, 4112 Gaston Avenue, Dallas, Texas. The Back to the Bible Broadcast, Box 233, Lincoln, Nebraska, publishes a similar course of study on a number of the books of the Bible, and these we heartily recommend.

A number of good Bible institutes, such as the Moody Bible Institute, 820 N. LaSalle St., Chicago 10, Illinois, have helpful correspondence courses of Bible study. These courses cover various books and portions of Scripture and a variety of themes. They are inexpensive, and a certificate of cred....

given for every course properly completed, which is an added incentive.

In these days when so few people are really familiar with the Holy Bible, and when a thorough knowledge of it is so essential, will you, my reader, accept the challenge to study the Word of God and be a REAL CHRISTIAN?

CHAPTER VIII

YOUR TESTIMONY TO OTHERS

Open Confession

It is impossible to live the Christian life in secret, although some erroneously attempt to do so. Life must manifest itself, wherever it is or whatever its nature. The new life which is imparted to every believer at his acceptance of Christ as Saviour must manifest itself outrightly. The only way to live a successful Christian life is to live it out in the open, without shame and without fear. If you desire to live a real Christian life, confess your Saviour and your faith in Him and love for Him openly before the world. Do not try to hide your Christianity. Put it up on a candlestick, that it may be un-hidden, like the city set on a hill. *Not only are you to show Christ in your life before men, but you are also to confess Him openly with your lips.*

Why must Christ be audibly confessed? To begin with, Christ himself commanded us to confess Him thus. Here is what He said: "Whosoever therefore shall confess me before men, him will I confess also before my Father which is in heaven" (Matt. 10:32). He demands a public confession from us. This is the path of blessing, for it is as He confesses us at the throne of God the Father, which is contingent upon our confession of Him down here, that the fullness of His blessing comes. So it is actually for our own sakes that He requires this confession on our part.

In Romans 10:9,10 the Spirit says, "If thou shalt confess with thy mouth Jesus as Lord, and shalt believe in thine heart that God raised him from the dead, thou shalt be saved: for with the heart man believeth unto righteousness; and with the mouth confession is made unto salvation" (R.V.). Audible confession of the Saviour is thus seen to be very important. To fail in this is to disobey and fail the Lord. It is to miss the fullness of salvation.

In the second place, we should confess Christ openly, because it is such a source of help and strength in our own Christian lives. Every time a Christian confesses Christ, he is strengthened spiritually. A witnessing Christian is not in much danger of backsliding, but failure to thus witness is a very frequent cause of backsliding. It is at this very point that the backsliding of many begins. Public testimony makes one strong, and, furthermore, it is a source of genuine joy. Though it may appear rather difficult to give an open testimony of your Christian faith at first, such testifying will always result in unspeakable joy. Many young converts who trembled with timidity and fear as they attempted their first testimonies for Christ overflowed with joy after their witness was given. It is a real source of inner strength and joy.

Moreover, a clear confession of one's faith before others solves a lot of problems. When worldly and ungodly people know that a person is out-and-out for Christ, they will stop trying to urge him to go to non-Christian amusements and to participate in unholy activities. Let them know right from the start where you stand, and you will be saved a lot of embarrassment and grief. The world may not love an out-and-out Christian, but it will always respect him. On the other hand, wishy-washy Christians are never taken seriously and are constantly being coaxed to go places and do things that even the world recognizes as not becoming to a real Christian. Thus, bold confession is a means of victory in Christian living.

Is it not really logical, in fact, inevitable, that you should unashamedly confess before men a Saviour who has done such great things for you? When some friend does us an outstanding act of kindness or a great favor, are we ashamed or reluctant to make it known? Do we not rather seek every possible opportunity to tell people about it? Rather than be ashamed to own such friends before others, we are proud to do so. Should it not be the same with our Friend who laid down His life to save us from our sins and from hell? If a child has a faithful, loving, and provident father, is it natural for that child to be ashamed of him or reluctant to confess him as his father? Are not children usually proud to do so? Should a wife be ashamed to make known who her husband is? If he is a good husband, she is happy and proud to acknowledge him as her own and to talk to people about him. We, as Christians, are called in the Bible the "bride" of Christ. Are we ashamed of Him or afraid to confess Him?

People who know that you are a Christian expect you to have a testimony for Christ. If they detect that you are ashamed of your Christianity, they certainly will never respect you as a real Christian. They will regard your Christian faith as weak and your Christian experience as unreal. They will not know how to catalogue you. But they know in which category to put a bold, witnessing Christian. They also know where to put the non-Christian. If you want to be regarded as a Christian, yet fear to confess your faith openly, the world is puzzled as to what pidgeonhole is yours. Why occasion them this difficulty? Why cause such difficulty for yourself and such grief to your Lord?

How should one confess Christ before people? First of all, take a public stand in some Christian assembly, such as a regular church service or some other gospel gathering. If you accepted Christ when you were by yourself or in your own home or place of business, as the case may have been, and did not take a public stand at that time, you should make such a profession at the very first opportunity. To walk forward in a public Christian gathering and take an open stand for Christ is an essential part of your confession.

It is not enough to make such a confession only once. You must confess Christ constantly. Never be ashamed to speak for Him and let people know to whom you belong, both in private life and in open testimony meetings. In the church, in the home, at work, at school, at play, always let people know where you stand. It goes without saying, of course, that your testimony must always be with humility. Any degree of pride will void your witness. My wife, as a convert in her teens, vowed in her heart that she would never sit through a testimony meeting without giving her testimony to Christ's salvation and what He meant to her. May I suggest that you formulate a like purpose right now?

Baptism is primarily a public confession that we have experienced cleansing from our sins. The waters of baptism, which only touch the outer surface of our physical being, were never designed to wash away sin which is within the heart and spirit, but the whole ceremony is a glorious symbol of our death to the old life of sin and our "resurrection" to a new life in Christ and a cleansing by His blood (Heb. 9:14; Rev. 1:5). (For a scriptural study of the true significance of baptism, examine Romans 6). According to Scripture, people are not baptized in order to be saved, but because they are saved.

The Lord commanded His followers to "baptize" all of those

whom they made disciples (Matt. 28:19). In the early church, from the very beginning at Pentecost, all of those who accepted Christ as their Saviour were baptized. It was by baptism that they signified, or confessed, their identity with Jesus Christ and His followers.

Baptism, then, being the personal command of Christ and the original practice of all His followers, as well as being an initial, public confession of Christ as Saviour to people around us, is not an insignificant or unimportant thing. It is obligatory to every Christian. It is not a matter of personal choice but of divine injunction. So to every believer, including the one who submitted meaninglessly to the ordinance before he was converted, we say, present yourself to a sound minister or church for public Christian baptism. I hold scriptural baptism to be by immersion.

Church membership should logically go along with public baptism and confession. Since we shall discuss that later, let this simple, single statement suffice here. God's children should not seek to play the role of the lone wolf or the wandering sheep.

Confess Christ faithfully, first, to your relatives and your friends. Begin in your Jerusalem—your own home circle. How can you expect to live a true Christian life if you do not let those who are closest to you know that you now belong to Christ? Let them hear of Christ from your lips and see Christ in your life. If you fail here, among those closest to you, you will not be strong in the Lord elsewhere. If to speak of Christ to your intimates means the loss of their friendship, then remember that such people are not true friends, after all. *How could one who stands in the way of your spiritual welfare be a real friend?*

Confess Christ clearly among all of your acquaintances and

associates. Never be afraid or ashamed. Make Him known to all with whom you come in contact. Let them all know that you love and serve Christ. Let it never be said by anyone with whom you were in contact, either in this life or in eternity, "He never told me about Jesus!" Let not such an indictment ever come against you, my Christian friend!

Jesus plainly told His disciples that they were to be His "witnesses" (Luke 24:48; Acts 1:8). They regarded themselves as such and faithfully filled that role (Acts 5:29-39; 10:39). This title is actually a legal term, a court word. In the light of this, what does the term really mean? What is a witness?

A witness is one who knows something. No one will ever be called up to the witness stand who does not know something about the case in hand. He must know something positively, definitely, personally. His knowledge must be that of personal contact, through one of his five physical senses. He must have seen something, heard something, felt something, tasted something, or smelled something. A witness cannot give opinions or deductions. He must relate what he knows to be the facts through his own senses, through personal experience and contact. *To be a witness for Christ, one must know something by personal contact.*

1. You must know by personal experience that you are saved before you can bear effective witness to anyone else that Jesus saves. Remember, the testimony of any witness may be cross-examined by some point-blank questions. Can you bear testimony that you know that Jesus saves, because you know that you are saved? Is your knowledge of His salvation personal, positive, and real? If your testimony is uncertain and indefinite, it will not convince people.

2. You must know by personal experience that God answers prayer, if you would testify to others of that fact.

Has God answered definite and personal petitions for you? Can you look back upon experiences of answered prayer, experiences that no one can contradict? Unless you can, how can you convince others? If you say that your teacher thinks so, or that the church teaches it, or merely that Christians have always believed it, you will never convince your friends that God answers prayer. But if you can relate personal experiences, they will constitute a positive testimony—one that will carry weight and convince the anxious soul. (No one can convince an arguing skeptic.)

3. You must know by your own experience that Christ can satisfy all the inner longings of the human heart before you can bear unfaltering testimony to others to that effect. They may not believe the beautiful phrases in the hymn book, they may not even accept the promises in the Bible, such as Matthew 11:28-30 and John 7:37-39, but they may believe you if you testify from real experience. Has Christ satisfied your longings? Can you testify out of your own experience? If so, your testimony will convince others; if not, it will bear little weight. However, we are sure that if you learn to trust Christ and take all of your problems to Him as they arise, you will learn that He can and does satisfy the longing soul with perfect peace and joy and rest.

4. You must know personally that Christ gives victory over sin, if you would convince your friends of that fact. Have you found victory over sin through Him, by prayer and faith? Has He given you some definite victories over besetting sins, and are you enjoying such victory now? When you try to lead a soul to Christ, you often hear something like this: "I'm afraid I couldn't hold out." Can you then come up with a clear, bold, unfaltering testimony to the victory-giving power of Christ in your life? Such a testimony will bear far more weight than

a sermon preached from the pulpit, no matter how brilliant or eloquent.

A witness is one who is willing to tell what he knows. One who is unwilling to tell that which he knows, no matter how well he knows it or how important it is, is not a witness. A witness must speak up. He must be willing to declare what he personally knows and also to answer any questions put to him. It is tragic to remain silent when it is imperative to speak. Imagine a man's remaining silent while another is being condemned to death in court, when he knows facts that would mean that person's exoneration, if he would but give his testimony! Surely no decent person would be guilty of such tragic silence.

In Ezekiel 33:8 we read as follows: "When I say unto the wicked, O wicked man, thou shalt surely die; if thou dost not speak to warn the wicked from his way, that wicked man shall die in his iniquity; but his blood will I require at thine hand." This is a solemn warning. As witnesses of God's saving grace to lost sinners, we cannot, we dare not, hold our peace. We must tell that which we know. God, grant that every Christian reading these lines will open his mouth boldly as a true witness for Jesus Christ and tell other people what he has come to know in his own heart and life! A witness must speak. He must tell what he knows. Are you one of Christ's "witnesses"?

A witness must live so that his testimony cannot be impeached. The personal character of any court witness largely determines the worth and weight of his testimony to the jury. If the witness is known in the community as an unreliable person, the jury will not attach much weight to his testimony. But if he is a man whose uprightness and honesty are known throughout his community and by all who know him, his words will bear tremendous weight. In courtrooms eager lawyers of the opposition watch every opportunity to pick out flaws in the character of a witness, even by calling attention to any previous instances of infidelity, thus undermining his testimony. So it is with the Christian in the world. Our walk must conform to our words. We cannot profess one thing and live another. Our lives must be true, if people are to hold our words as true.

One time in a revival meeting a professing Christian approached an unconverted man about accepting Christ. The sinner caustically sneered, "Say, Jim, what about your affair with old Widow Brown?" (He had wronged and cheated an aged widow.) Jim's face turned red, and he said, "Oh, that was business. This is religion." Needless to say, he did not win the man to Christ.

Strive to keep true and clean. When you sin, go to Christ immediately for forgiveness and cleansing. If you should offend any person, go to him, apologize, and ask his pardon. If you practice this, people will honor your life and believe your testimony. Take your Bible right now and read Titus 2:7,8; I Peter 2:11,12,15; I Peter 3:15,16; Acts 4:13. Ponder these verses and seek to carry them out in your life.

A witness never retracts his testimony. Once the testimony is given, he stands by it. He will never alter his word or compromise his own witness. To do so would be fatal to his effectiveness and would make him the object of disregard and disbelief. The Greek word "witness," in the New Testament, is the one from which our word *martyr* comes. A true witness will die for his testimony. He will never alter or retract it.

Many Christians in the past have died for the witness of Jesus—thousands and thousands of them. They were burned at the stake, they were put in boiling tar, they were thrown to wild beasts in public arenas, they were crucified, they were pulled in two, they had their tongues cut out, they had their eyes burned with hot irons, and they were broken on the "wheel"; but they would not retract their testimony, and they died singing His praises.

Christian converts in Moslem lands still suffer and die because of their witness for Christ. They also suffer in communistic countries and in many pagan lands. And here in our own country some are ready to "pull in their feathers" when they meet just a little ridicule. Shame on us! Let us be faithful witnesses for Christ, even as He was once on earth a faithful witness for us and still is at the right hand of the throne of God (Rev. 1:5).

Chapter IX

YOUR RESPONSIBILITY

Winning Others

In the fifth chapter of II Corinthians, beginning with verse 15, we read, "He died for all, that they which live should not henceforth live unto themselves, but unto him which died for them, and rose again . . . and all things are of God, who hath reconciled us to himself by Jesus Christ, and hath given to us the ministry of reconciliation . . . Now then we are ambassadors for Christ, as though God did beseech you by us: we pray you in Christ's stead, be ye reconciled to God."

Notice, primarily, in these verses that we who are Christians are ambassadors for Christ and that the ministry of reconciling men to God has been committed to us. We are the ones who, in Christ's stead, are now to go out and prevail upon men to be reconciled unto God. Only as we reconcile men to God by preaching to them the gospel of the grace of the Lord Jesus Christ will they ever be saved. This is our responsibility —this is our task here on earth.

He who would be a real Christian must be an ambassador for Christ. An ambassador for Christ is one who goes out in His stead and beseeches men to be reconciled unto God through Him. The task of every Christian is to win others to Christ. If you want to live a real Christian life, one that is pleasing unto God, put your hand to the plow of soul-winning.

There is a beautiful tribute paid in the first chapter of John to Andrew, after he had found Jesus as his Messiah and Saviour: "He first findeth his own brother Simon, and saith unto him, We have found the Messias!" From the very hour when Andrew himself became a follower of the Lord Jesus Christ, he had a desire to go and bring others, and he began by winning his own brother to the Lord. Signally, his brother (Peter) became a more influential disciple of the Lord than Andrew himself and rendered a more important service. This can be an encouragement to you. You may think yourself a very influential and humble Christian, yet you might win someone to Christ who will be the means of reaching thousands for the Lord.

The person who led D. L. Moody to Christ, for instance, did not realize that he was leading to the Saviour a man who in turn would bring thousands to Him. If you want to be a real Christian, follow Andrew's example. Start out by trying to win others to Christ, and begin with your own family. Notice how simple Andrew's testimony was. He simply said, "We have found the Messiah." You could go to your friends and loved ones and say, "I have found the Saviour." Is that difficult to do? Is that beyond your ability? Who knows but what your saying to someone, "I have found the Saviour," may result in that one's salvation, even as Andrew's testimony resulted in Simon Peter's salvation?

Let me pass on a statement from the Apostle Paul, found in the fourth chapter of Ephesians. I quote from Dr. Weymouth's translation of the New Testament: "And he himself appointed some to be apostles, some to be prophets, some to be evangelists, some to be pastors and teachers, in order to fully equip his people for the work of serving—for the building up of Christ's body—till we all of us arrive at oneness of faith and in the knowledge of the Son of God and that mature manhood and the stature of full grown men in Christ" (Eph. 4:11-13). Notice here that the great Head of the Church, Jesus Christ, has given to every Christian some gift or ability. And there is a task for every one of them to fulfill. This verse says that He has given various gifts to different Christians "in order to fully equip His people for the work of serving."

You are equipped to serve in some part of Christ's work, the winning of souls. And notice that the ultimate aim of all this is the building up of Christ's Body. In Williams' recent modern English translation of the New Testament this phrase reads, "For the ultimate building up of the body of Christ." As Christians all over the world engage in the task of winning men to Jesus Christ, the Body of Christ will ultimately be built up—that is, be completed. Then, when the last necessary soul is won, Jesus will come back again! What an incentive to go out and try to win men to Him! Who knows but what it will be your personal privilege to win the last one, and then the Lord will come and catch us up together to be with Him in the air!

In the previous chapter we said a great deal about giving audible testimony to your faith in Christ. We wish now to say that the one primary object of your testimony should be to win others to the Lord. Of course, it is true that we want to confess the Lord Jesus Christ down here on earth, in order that He may confess us up in heaven at His Father's right hand; but on the other hand, the thing which pleases the Lord most and which should be the greatest desire of our own hearts is that we might be the means of bringing other souls to Him.

As we notice in the quotation from II Corinthians 5, we are not to live unto ourselves, for our own personal pleasures and pursuits, but rather for Christ. And the life that is most pleasing to Christ is the life that is dedicated to winning lost souls to Him. When He told His disciples, in the first chapter of Acts, that they were to be His witnesses, even unto the uttermost part of the earth, the great object of that witness was that they might win men and women to Jesus Christ from every kindred and tongue and people and nation.

When you came to Christ as a lost sinner, no doubt the main object of your coming was that your own soul might be saved; but now that you are saved, the object of your life ought to be the salvation of others. No less object or goal becomes you as a Christian or pleases your Lord. The reason why Christ is so eager to have us confess Him before men is that through our confession other men might come to know Him as their Saviour.

If the Lord did not have such an object in our life here on earth, it would be better for Him to take us on to heaven just as soon as we are saved, for that would save us much heartache, and it would also save Him much grief. But He has a purpose for us here on earth. He wants our lights to shine before men, so that others who are now in darkness may come to know Him as their God. If you are a young Christian, God has great purposes in store for your life, and if He allows you to live long upon the earth, it will only be for this purpose— that through you many may come to know Him. If you are already well along in years and have known the Lord for a long time, the one object He has had in sparing your life thus far is simply that others, through your life, might have come to know Him. Has that purpose been realized in your life? Or have you disappointed your Saviour?

In the fifteenth chapter of John's gospel we have our Lord's beautiful illustration of our relationship to Him—that of the vine and the branches. He says in that chapter, verse 5, "I am the vine, ye are the branches: He that abideth in me, and I in him, the same bringeth forth much fruit: for without me ye can do nothing."

The chief lesson He is pointing out through this figure is that of His indispensability to us. As the vine is indispensable to the branch, so Christ is indispensable to His people. He says, "Without me ye can do nothing." As the branch can do nothing without the vine, so we can do nothing without Christ. He is indispensable to our soul's salvation. He is indispensable to our spiritual fruitfulness. He is indispensable to our spiritual life and health. He is indispensable to our strength. It is easy to catch this truth in His illustration.

But on the other hand, there is another truth taught very subtly in this same illustration. It is that *the branch is also indispensable to the vine.* As the branch cannot bear fruit without the vine, neither can the vine bear fruit without the branch. Fruit is always produced on the branches of the tree, never on the vine or trunk. This is God's order both in nature and in the spiritual realm. Remember that Christ said, "Ye are the branches." That means that we are also indispensable to Him. He cannot bear fruit without us. By fruit we mean other souls brought to Christ. It is only through us, as branches of the Vine, that other men and women can come to know the Saviour. We are His indispensable instruments.

All the work that Christ is doing in the world now and has been doing ever since Pentecost, He has been doing through His people. The Holy Spirit dwells in the people of

God, in the Christians, and all of His work is done through them. It is only as Christians pray, as Christians witness, as Christians preach, as Christians talk to people about the Saviour, that souls can be saved. If every Christian in the world would cease to function for God, the whole work of Christ's spiritual kingdom on earth would come to a standstill.

We are indispensable to Him and to His work. The only way in which souls can be won to Christ now is through the witness and instrumentality of Christians. If we do not win men to Christ, they will not be won. If we do not bear testimony to the saving grace of Christ, no testimony will be borne. If we do not proclaim the gospel, it will not be proclaimed. If we do not evangelize the world, it will not be evangelized. The only feet that Christ has to carry His gospel in the world today are our feet. The only tongue He has to proclaim His gospel to lost men is our tongue. The only lips He has today to tell the story of His saving grace and His atoning death on Calvary's cross are our lips. The only hands He has to translate the Scriptures into other languages are our hands. The only witness He has among men of His mercy and grace is our witness. How dare we fail Him?

It may seem a bit difficult at first to begin this ministry of soul-winning, but once you have won a soul to Christ, you will never want to stop. The evangelist D. L. Moody made it the rule of his life never to let one day pass without speaking to someone about salvation and trying to win that one to Christ. A person does not have to be either eloquent or "clever" to win souls.

In your talking to men and women about their souls, the greatest problem seems to be how to open up the conversation. One way to do this is to carry some good gospel tracts with you and pass them out whenever the opportunity arises. The giving out of a tract will open the way for a conversation concerning salvation. Then you can tell the person how you were saved, and you can assure him that Christ will save him, too, if he will only accept Him as you did.

Another good way is to have some little pin on your garment, perhaps on the lapel of your coat, which will attract the attention of people and cause them to ask questions. I once wore a fairly prominent gold question mark on the lapel of my coat, made specially for me by a jeweler. When people would ask what the question mark stood for, I would ask, "Well, what is the most important question in the world?" Then I would go on to say that I consider the question, "Are you saved?" to be the biggest question in life.

A friend of ours wore a gold "3" on his lapel, and whenever people asked him what it stood for, he would tell them, "The Trinity—the Father, the Son, and the Holy Ghost." Then he would go on to explain how God the Father loved men, how Christ, His Son, died for men, and how the Holy Spirit waits to come into the heart of anyone who will accept the Saviour, and He will transform his life.

R. A. Torrey, Jr. once related to us the great joy which he experienced when he led his first soul to Christ. He was in the choir loft during a meeting in which his father was preaching, and while the invitation was being given, the preacher urged the people from the choir to go down into the audience and try to lead souls to the altar and to Christ. Young Torrey sat stupefied until the song leader pushed him down the steps of the platform and said, "Go and get a soul." With a great deal of embarrassment and timidity, he stopped at the first young man he came to and asked him if he would like to come to

Christ. To his amazement, the fellow responded by starting toward Torrey at once and making his way to the altar. Reuben Torrey, Jr. led that young man to Christ, and he testified that it was the greatest experience in his spiritual life since the hour he himself had been saved. So it will be with you, my reader. Once the ministry of soul-winning is begun, it will be the joy and desire of your life to win others to the Saviour.

The most convincing thing in your testimony as you try to win others to Christ will be a genuine love in your heart for them. People almost always respond to love, and when they see that you really have a love and concern for their souls, they will not be bitter when you try to lead them to Christ. By speaking to them in love, you may win them to the Saviour. If you do not have such love in your heart for the souls of men, pray to the Holy Spirit of God for Him to shed the love of God abroad in your heart, for that is one of His ministries in the life of every Christian (Rom. 5:5). While we cannot make ourselves love and cannot fill our own hearts with love for lost souls, the Holy Spirit is able, willing, and glad to do it, when we ask Him, and as we allow Him. Any effort to win a soul to Christ which stems from genuine love for that soul, though it may be a faulty effort, will not fail to make its impression upon that one and, more likely than not, will result in his salvation.

A real Christian is a soul-winning Christian. No soul-winning Christian ever becomes a backslider. No soul-winning Christian ever is overcome by discouragement. No soul-winning Christian is an unhappy Christian. No soul-winning Christian is a defeated Christian.

Of course, a life of prayer is the secret behind all soul-winning. If we start about the task of soul-winning without praying that God may really bless our efforts and enable us to win men for Christ, our efforts will end in failure. But as we pray to Him for real power, grace, and love in our lives, so that we can win souls, and then go out sincerely purposing to bring our friends and acquaintances to the Saviour, our efforts will be abundantly rewarded.

If you would be a real Christian, be a soul-winner. Begin at once. Begin on your knees in the prayer room, and then deal with the first person whom you meet outside the prayer room who needs your Saviour.

Chapter X

YOUR RELATIONSHIP TO THE WORLD

Perhaps the greatest test in the Christian's life comes in the matter of his relationship to the world. It seems hard for some Christians to let go of certain worldly things that hold them down and hinder them from making spiritual progress. It seems too easy for them to hold on to things that are barriers to spiritual growth.

I remember going into a restaurant one time where there was a machine for testing how much electrical current one could stand—a fool's gadget for sure. There was a pair of "hot" grips on this machine, and the closer you drew these grips together, the stronger the current became. On a central panel was a dial to indicate how much current you were getting, the idea, of course, being to outdo the other fellow. After several of my companions had taken hold of the grips, had drawn them slowly together and had let go again, I stepped up to the machine. I had meanwhile decided that instead of drawing the handles together slowly, I would just force them together with one big push. I did this, but to my amazement, the current became so strong that I was unable to let go! What an experience it was! There I stood with the electricity coursing through my body, being hurt by it, but unable to let go.

That is exactly the way it is with so many things of the world. While the person holding on is conscious of the fact that he is being hurt, he seemingly cannot let go. The world burns spiritual hands, but it also grips. No honest person can deny its grip.

There are various passages of Scripture which speak of the Christian's relationship to the world. Jesus said, "Ye are not of the world" (John 15:19). Paul says in Titus 2:12, "Teaching us that, *denying ungodliness and worldly lusts,* we should live soberly, righteously, and godly, in this present world." In the second chapter of his epistle to the Ephesians, the same apostle says, in verse 2, referring to the time previous to their conversion, "Wherein in time past ye walked according to the course of this world, according to the prince of the power of the air, the spirit that now worketh in the children of disobedience." Then farther on in the chapter, in verses 12 and 13, he continues, "That at that time ye were without Christ ... without God in the world: but now in Christ Jesus ye who sometimes were far off are made nigh by the blood of Christ." There is a tremendous contrast here pointed out before and after these people were saved. Before they were saved, they followed the course of this world and the desires of the evil one, but now since they have come to know Christ, this has been changed.

In II Timothy 4:10 the apostle writes: "For Demas hath forsaken me, having loved this present world, and is departed." In James 4:4 we have this strong statement, "Ye adulterers and adulteresses, know ye not that the friendship of the world is enmity with God? whosoever therefore will be a friend of the world is the enemy of God." And in the first epistle of John, chapter 2 and verse 15, notice these words: "Love not the world, neither the things that are in the world. If any man love the world, the love of the Father is not in him."

Permit one more quotation from the Word of God: "Wherefore come out from among them, and be ye separate, saith the Lord, and touch not the unclean thing; and I will receive you" (II Cor. 6:17).

He who would be a real Christian must hear and heed what the Word of God says regarding his relationship to this world of sin. When a person becomes a Christian and has experienced a transformation in his life, there must necessarily be a giving up of many things and ways and pleasures of the world. The reason for this is, as John states in his first epistle, chapter 5 and verse 19, "The whole world lieth in wickedness." Surely anyone who looks at this world with an unbiased mind can see that, on the whole, it has departed far from God, and it is full of all manner of uncleanness and evil. The people of the world loved wicked and impure things. Most of the pleasures of the world are associated with that which is unclean and impure, many of them positively vile and degrading.

The whole spirit of the world is a spirit of indifference to the things of God, if not positive hatred of Christ. The world's spirit is largely centered around the love of that which is unholy and base. The vile conversation of worldly people, the low standard of conduct of worldly people, and the sex-madness and immorality of the world are certainly no prizes for the Christian to covet. There is hardly a popular pleasure in the world's playhouses today that is not associated with that which is degrading. Almost everything purposely centers around crime, horror, and sex.

Surely every Christian realizes that with the standards of the world the way they are, he must draw the line somewhere. Where should he draw it? Now that you believe on the Lord Jesus Christ and are seeking to follow Him, you immediately find yourself face to face with certain pertinent questions.

Shall I go to the movies? Shall I play cards? Shall I continue to dance? Shall I smoke cigarettes? These and a host of other questions arise in your mind and demand a clear-cut answer. What shall the Christian's answer be? Enough has been written and said regarding all of these things to make long dissertations here superfluous. The author's own book, *The Perfect Will of God,"* previously published, devotes one chapter to the matter of the Christian's relationship to the world. Many other Christian writers have lent their pens, very ably, to the discussion of these questions.

We believe that any honest person must acknowledge that the motion picture theater is a place that glorifies crime, infidelity, and lust and that no red-blooded person can look upon the sex scenes constantly portrayed upon the screen without being affected by them in an unwholesome way. Many of the crimes and sex sins committed by young people today are due to the influence of the cinema. This is a fact that cannot be denied, and it is one of the constant claims of the Federal Bureau of Investigation of our government.

The men who control the motion picture industry are interested in one primary thing—making money. To that end they are anxious to produce on the screen such films as will draw in the greatest number of people, without any scruples about standards of decency, righteousness, or purity. So they keep going farther and farther along the pathway of lust, immorality, and crime. It is a pity that eighty million Americans weekly feed their systems upon the lustful and disgraceful motion picture films of our day.

Occasionally, of course, some films are interspersed which in themselves may be called good, but the purpose even in those is to reach that smaller group of more scrupulous people who do not attend the viler pictures, in an effort to get their money, too. Hollywood, where the films are produced, is the open cesspool of the world!

As for dancing, I think that the same admission must be made, that it is based mainly upon the sex appeal and that it aggravates the baser lusts of men. Though some may try to argue in favor of the dance, we believe that the case has long since been lost and that such argument is not only futile, but foolish. If anyone denies that dancing is not based upon sex and lust, let him try sponsoring a dance where men dance with men and women dance with women and see how well it goes over!

Cards have long been associated with gambling, even in the minds of little children. We feel that the rule for the Christian is "hands off." The boy who has been brought up in a home where no card-playing was indulged in or permitted is not likely to fall into the hands of gamblers when he grows into manhood; whereas the young man who was taught to play cards in the home could be an easy prey to the vice of gambling in later life.

As for the use of tobacco, at its best it is only a waste of money and a hindrance to the Christian testimony. At its worst it is a detriment to the human body, a hindrance to one's Christian testimony, and a vicious habit that can warp one's entire being. A habit that fixes itself upon a man like a leech and that has evil effects upon his physical organs and his nervous system certainly is not becoming for a child of God. Our bodies are temples of the Holy Ghost, and we should keep them as clean as possible for Him. We do not believe that the Holy Spirit takes delight in dwelling in a body that smells like a tobacco sack. If we proclaim to the world a Christ who is able to give men victory over their sins and evil habits and yet are ourselves enslaved to the cigarette, our testimony will surely be greatly weakened.

But do not get the impression that the Christian life is a dull one. Almost always in the Scriptures when separation is referred to, it is not only a separation "from" but also a separation "unto." We are separated from the world unto God. In place of everything the Lord takes out of our lives, He gives us something far better. The more we find ourselves separated unto the things of Christ, the less appeal the things of the world will have for us. We will find ourselves automatically separated from those things. The last night Jesus was with His disciples before the crucifixion, He pointed out to them that though they were in the world, they were not of the world. This is exactly our position as Christians in this world. He has chosen us from among the people of the world and has separated us unto Himself as His own peculiar people. The Church means the "called-out" group, because it has been called out and separated from the world. We ought to so live in this world that all men will understand that we have been called out from it and that we are a people separated unto God.

If we follow the world in all of its ways, do what the world does, feed upon what the world feeds upon, pattern our lives after the world's standards, how shall men know that we are Christ's disciples? But when they see a difference between our lives and their own, they will know that we have been with Jesus. This is what we want.

Is the price too great to pay? God is leaving us in this world so that we might be the means of lighting the way for other men. Hence, it is not for us to seclude ourselves in monasteries or withdraw ourselves utterly apart from the people of the world, but to live like children of God in the midst of a world filled with wickedness and to "shew forth the praises" of Him who has called us out of darkness into His marvelous light."

After all, the world is a very empty and unsatisfying place. If you will study the Book of Ecclesiastes, in the Old Testament, you will see how Solomon tried everything the world could offer but found no satisfaction or peace in it. He came to the conclusion that it was all "vanity." In the first chapter of the book he calls attention, beginning with verse 13, to the fact that he sought out education and wisdom, thinking that human knowledge would satisfy the thirst of his inner being. But he came to the conclusion that this was all "vexation of spirit" and "vanity."

At the beginning of chapter two he states how he then turned to mirth and pleasure, indulging in all of the pleasures of the world to the full. But this he found was also vanity. Then a little farther down in the same chapter, in fact, throughout the rest of the book, he shows how he tried to satisfy the longings of his heart with the wealth of the world. He secured everything that money could buy, thinking that this would surely bring him satisfaction, but his conclusion of the whole thing was that all is "vanity and vexation of spirit."

Surely if any man was ever in a position to test the world out to the full, Solomon was. And if the world could not by its pleasures and knowledge and wealth bring satisfaction to a great man like Solomon, it surely cannot do so to any of us. Those who have followed the ways of the world long enough will have come to the same conclusion that Solomon came to —that it is all empty and void. What shall it profit a man if he gain the whole world and lose his own soul?

The world strongly allures and gives promise of bringing satisfaction to men, but it is disillusioning and deceitful. It cannot keep its promises. It will leave the life unsatisfied and the soul cold and hungry. Often those who have attained the largest amount of the world's wealth and pleasure are the ones who end their lives in suicide. Why, then, should the Christian set his affections upon such an empty and false world?

It is rather for the Christian, as Paul says in Colossians 3:1, to "seek those things which are above, where Christ sitteth on the right hand of God. Set your affection on things above, not on things on the earth." Where one's treasure is, there will his heart be also. If our treasure is in heaven, our affections will be set upon heavenly things; but, of course, if our treasure is here on earth, our affections will be directed to the things of earth. Where is your treasure? Where should your affections be? The Apostle John said, "Love not the world, neither the things that are in the world. If any man love the world, the love of the Father is not in him" (I John 2:15). Here again the same thought is brought out. If the love of God has entered our hearts and is flooding our souls, we will love not the things of the world that reject and hate Christ, but rather the things above, where Christ is. So the problem of our relationship to the world is, after all, a problem of our relationship to Christ. If our relationship to Christ is right, our relationship to the world becomes automatic.

There are a few questions which I would like to pass on to you, Christian friend, which may be of help to you. In deciding whether you should or should not do a certain thing, ask yourself these questions:

1. Is this pleasing to Christ?

2. Does it glorify God?

3. Would Jesus do it?

4. Will it strengthen my testimony to others as a Christian?

5. Will it help me in my own Christian life?

If the answer to these questions is in the negative, turn your back immediately upon the thing in question. If the answer is positive, then proceed.

It should also be borne in mind that some Christians might go to certain places, do certain things, and be the means of winning men to Christ by so doing, whereas other Christians going to those same places would only be stumbling blocks. So sometimes what is right for one Christian may be entirely wrong for another. And for that reason, always apply these five test questions to anything about which you are in doubt. We believe that they will prove to be the acid test, and by them almost every question or problem regarding your relationship to the world can be settled.

God says to us, "Whatsoever ye do, do it heartily, as to the Lord, and not unto men; knowing that of the Lord ye shall receive the reward of the inheritance: for ye serve the Lord Christ" (Col. 3:23, 24). In the same chapter, a few verses above, verse 17, we read a stronger statement: "And whatsoever ye do in word or deed, do all in the name of the Lord Jesus, giving thanks to God and the Father by him." In I Corinthians 10:31 we read, "Whatsoever ye do, do all to the glory of God. Give none offence, neither to the Jews, nor to the Gentiles, nor to the church of God."

If you cannot go to the theater in the name of Christ, to the glory of God, and without giving offense to your testimony, do not go. If you cannot dance in the name of Jesus, to the glory of God, without offense to anyone, do not dance. If you cannot play cards in the name of Jesus, to the glory of God, without offense to anyone, do not play cards. If you cannot smoke cigarettes in the name of Jesus, to the glory of God, without offending anybody, do not smoke. Instead of asking the question, "Is it wrong to do this?" why not ask, "Is it to the glory of God? Can I do it heartily as unto the Lord? Can I do it in the name of Jesus?"

As Christians, we should not be interested in seeing how close we can get to the fire without being burned, but how far we can keep from danger. The Scripture says that we should "abstain from all appearance of evil." Why not stay on the safe side of the fence and make a clean break with every worldly thing that might hinder your spiritual life and your testimony for Christ?

CHAPTER XI

YOUR INNER HELPER

The Holy Spirit

In the chapters immediately preceding this one we have brought to you some of the great challenges of the Christian life. Perhaps you have been tempted to think that all of this is a bit too difficult for you and that you can never live that kind of a Christian life. You are perhaps tempted to think that you never can be a REAL CHRISTIAN.

If it were up to us personally to attain such goals spiritually as we have been pointing out, it would, naturally, be impossible. In our own human strength we could never live such Christian lives. But we are not left to our own strength and resources for living the Christian life. We have a competent Inner Helper, a Personal Enabler, the Person of the Holy Spirit.

The Lord Jesus, before He went away, repeatedly promised to His disciples the coming of the Holy Spirit to abide in them and to strengthen them in their life on earth for God. He said, "I will pray the Father, and he shall give you another Comforter, that he may abide with you for ever; Even the Spirit" (John 14:16,17); "When the Comforter is come, whom I will send unto you from the Father, even the Spirit of truth, which proceedeth from the Father, he shall testify of me: And ye also shall bear witness" (John 15:26,27); "If I go not away, the Comforter will not come unto you;

but if I depart, I will send him unto you" (John 16:7).

In I Corinthians 3:16 we read, "Know ye not that ye are the temple of God, and that the Spirit of God dwelleth in you?" In 6:19 of the same book we read, "What? know ye not that your body is the temple of the Holy Ghost which is in you, which ye have of God, and ye are not your own?" The Apostle Paul confidently prayed for the Ephesian converts that they might be "strengthened with might by his Spirit in the inner man," in order that they might attain unto a spiritual fullness in the Christian life.

The Holy Spirit is our Inner Helper, and by His power and strength we are able to meet all the challenges that come to us as Christians and to succeed in living a real Christian life. What is to our natural strength utterly impossible is by His power definitely and easily possible. The words of Christ in John 14:18, in connection with the coming of the Holy Spirit, in the Greek literally are, "I will not leave you orphans." Without the inner strength of God's Holy Spirit to fit us to live the Christian life as God has pointed it out and to enable us to face its challenges and assume its responsibilities, we would be like helpless, orphaned children. The Lord Jesus knew this very well. Therefore, as He bids farewell to His disciples on His last night on earth, He promises them the coming of God's Holy Spirit to dwell in them and to strengthen them for their Christian life and service.

The promise of the Holy Spirit's indwelling is the heritage of every Christian. When one is born again, he is "born of the Spirit." In other words, when one is born of God, it is really the Holy Spirit coming into his soul and implanting the life of God in him thus by his own Personal Presence. By the strength and power of that Holy Spirit we are not helpless to live in this world as God expects us to live.

There are many things in the Bible, both in the words of Christ and the words of His apostles, which are promised to us through the Presence and Power of the Holy Spirit.

1. The Holy Spirit helps our infirmities (Rom. 8:26). We have many weaknesses and infirmities, but He is ever present to meet our deficits and supply the strength where we lack. So even the weakest and most infirm Christian may take courage when he remembers that the Holy Spirit has come to meet all human infirmities and to overcome them with His divine strength.

2. He gives us understanding of the truths of the Bible (John 16:12,13). We have already called attention to the fact that the understanding of the Bible comes, not through human intellect, but by divine enlightenment. It is the mission of the Holy Spirit to guide God's people into divine truth. So when you read the Bible, read it in communion with the Holy Spirit. Read it on your knees. When you come to passages that you do not understand, pause and ask Him to give you the interpretation. He is the author of the Scriptures (II Pet. 1:20, 21), and He is its interpreter.

3. He gives us love (Rom. 5:5). Love is our most vital need—love to God, love to our fellow Christians, and love to all men. The first and greatest commandment of all under the dispensation of law in the Old Testament was that men should love the Lord their God with all their heart, and the greatest point of emphasis under the dispensation of grace in the New Testament is the same. After Peter had denied Jesus, the Lord's question to him was simply, "Lovest thou me?" To His disciples He challengingly said, "By this shall all men know that ye are my disciples, if ye love one another." One of the great lacks in the Christian world today is the lack of love between Christians. This is a serious lack, and it is

one of the great stumbling blocks to the world. Unless we manifest the love of Christ to sinful people around us, how can we ever win them to Christ?

Love is unquestionably our greatest need and our greatest lack. For a study of this matter of love on the part of the Christian, go to the First Epistle of John.

We cannot make ourselves love, but the Holy Spirit will shed the love of God abroad in our hearts, if we let Him do so. So, then, when we are conscious of a coldness and a lack of love in our hearts, let us seek the Holy Spirit's love-shedding ministry. As we are filled with the Holy Spirit, we will be filled with the love of God. We can be filled with the Holy Spirit by simply yielding ourselves to Him and emptying our lives of every other thing. If we but yield ourselves to Him for His fullness and sincerely ask Him to fill us, He will not fail to do so.

4. He gives us strength against sin (Eph. 3:16). This inner strength which He is ever ready to supply will enable us to gain victory over sin. He enables us to defeat Satan. When you feel yourself being overcome by sin or slipping down into error, breathe a prayer to the indwelling Holy Spirit right then and there, and He will not fail to give you victory.

5. He aids us in prayer (Rom. 8:26, 27). He is the One, first of all, who impels us to pray. Christ intercedes for us in heaven before the Father on the throne, while the Holy Spirit intercedes within our hearts on earth. The Spirit frequently moves us to pray and lays heavy burdens upon our hearts for certain things or certain people. It is at just such times as this that you should cooperate carefully with the Spirit and yield yourself to His control, so that you may be led into a real life and ministry of prayer. The Holy Spirit also instructs us as to how we should pray and concerning that

for which we should pray. Many times we know not what we should pray for as we ought, but the Holy Spirit stirs up petitions in us with groanings which cannot be uttered.

We would of ourselves often ask for things which are pleasant and which seem good in our judgment but which would be far from best for us, so the Holy Spirit, who knows what is good and right for us, lays upon our hearts the very things for which we should pray. He comes to our aid. He begets holy desires within us for the things of God and for the glory of God, which we would never have in ourselves. He helps us to pray. He prays in us and through us.

Praying is not merely asking for natural desires which arise in our own mind, nor is it merely beautiful words of expression. *Real prayer is the Holy Spirit's begetting holy desires within us and then intensifying them to such an extent that we will not rest or cease praying until God has granted the petition.*

Satan attacks us in our prayer life more than in anything else, so right here is where we need a Helper. It is the Holy Spirit who gives us the desire to pray and who enables us to actually pray. When you find yourself unable to pray, then lean hard upon the Holy Spirit and ask Him to come to your rescue. It is one of His ministries to you, and He loves to perform it.

6. The Holy Spirit directs and leads in the lives of God's people (Rom. 8:14). Often we do not know what decision to make and cannot in ourselves determine the will of God. It is at such times as this that the Holy Spirit comes to our aid, willing to lead and guide in every detail of our lives, if we will only live close enough to Him so that He can do so. A Christian should cultivate the habit of asking the Holy Spirit to guide him every day of his life.

In the morning, when you arise, before you face your daily

tasks, breathe an earnest prayer to the Holy Spirit, asking Him to guide every thought, every decision, every step, every move of yours during that day. And then, throughout the hours of the day, as you go about your work, facing problems, needs, and dilemmas, lift your heart in prayer to the indwelling Holy Spirit for guidance. He has come to be your Guide, and He will not fail to give you direction and light.

7. It is the Holy Spirit who produces the heavenly fruits in the Christian's life (Gal. 5:22,23). It is the Holy Spirit who gives love. It is the Holy Spirit who fills your heart with joy. It is the Holy Spirit who gives you peace. It is the Holy Spirit who makes you patient. It is the Holy Spirit who makes you gentle. It is the Holy Spirit who enables Christians to live good lives. It is the Holy Spirit who imparts faith and increases your faith. It is the Holy Spirit who grants you the ability to be meek. It is the Holy Spirit who gives you the power to be temperate, to restrain your natural appetites and desires. All of the merits of the Christian life are imparted and ministered to us by the Blessed Holy Spirit. So learn to commune with the Holy Spirit, in order that He might impart these things unto you.

We are persuaded that there are many Christians to whom the Presence of the Holy Spirit is not real. That is a tragedy. The Holy Spirit is a Person as much as God the Father or Jesus Christ are Persons. And He indwells every Christian. If you will yield your life completely to Him, turning the reins of your entire course over to His hands, He will lead you into the abundant life. In the previous book, "The Perfect Will of God," we dealt more at length with the matter of the ministry of the Holy Spirit to the believer.

Learn to cultivate fellowship with the Holy Spirit. Think of Him as an Indwelling Presence, a real Person. Contemplate His gracious yearnings for your growth and spiritual prosperity. Consider His goodness, His graciousness, and His willingness to help you at every turn of the way. Learn to rely upon Him for all of your spiritual needs. Learn to talk to Him and to commune with Him. Learn to draw from Him all the spiritual graces that you desire to be manifested in your life, which God also desires. Think of Him as He really is—a Heavenly Guest, the Lover of your soul. He is your Friend, your Companion, your Comforter, your Guide, your Helper, your Teacher. Let Him be your All in All.

CHAPTER XII

YOUR WORSHIP

In Home and Church

Jesus said to the woman of Samaria, "God is a Spirit: and they that worship him must worship him in spirit and in truth" (John 4:24). The worship of God, to the Christian, is primarily spiritual exercise—that is to say, he worships God in his heart and should be constantly in the spirit of worship. But this does not eliminate the necessity of having special times set apart for the purpose of worship—times when all other activity is put aside. We can and ought to be worshipping God in our hearts unceasingly. We ought to be in a spirit of prayer constantly, yet there must be times when everything else is put aside for the sole purpose of worship and for prayer. There must be regular exercises of worship and a regular time for worship.

We have already spoken of our personal prayer life, so our present discussion will be confined to the worship of God in our homes and in the church.

The Family Altar

There may be some of our readers who do not quite know what we mean by the term "family altar," so let us explain before proceeding. By "family altar" we mean a time set apart every day in the home when the whole family engages in the worship of the Lord through reading the Bible and praying together. There is nothing we know of that can be a greater blessing in any home than family worship. Nothing will do more to instill the fear of God and the love of God in the hearts of children, and nothing will so completely eliminate family differences and troubles. When the family gets together, at least once a day, for prayer and worship, all ill feelings and unkind thoughts are swept away. No husband and wife can pray together daily without being in true harmony with each other. When differences do arise, they will either stop praying or else be shortly reconciled.

I feel that the family altar is indispensable to the home. No greater heritage can be left to the children of a Christian family than the recollection of their childhood days, when father and mother and children daily knelt around the Word of God and lifted their voices in united, audible prayer. In fact, we do not believe that a home can be a real Christian home unless it does have a family altar. There are many homes of Christians that are not essentially or truly Christian homes. This is deplorable but, nevertheless, true.

Now that you have become a Christian, begin family worship in your home at once. The way to begin family worship is to have a time set apart for it each day. Perhaps right after breakfast is the best time (or after supper). Begin by going through a certain book of the Bible, reading a chapter or a portion of a chapter each time. Then let all the family kneel together in prayer, with as many participating in prayer as possible. There may be days when there will be time for only father or mother to pray, but there should also be times when there will be ample opportunity for the children to take part in prayer. Every Christian in the family should participate. It is well worth while to take enough time for family worship, so that problems in the Bible text can be discussed as they are faced. At certain times children should be given an opportunity to ask any questions they may have upon their hearts.

Normally, the family altar should be conducted by the father, as the head of the house. But circumstances may make it necessary for others to lead at times. If the husband is not a Christian but is willing for the wife to conduct family worship, then she should by all means do so. One of the older children who has been converted might even take the lead in family worship, if the parents are willing. Normally, where both parents are Christians, the father should act as the priest of the family.

Where there are small children in the home, it might be good once a day at family worship to read from some Bible story book and give a few simple explanations of the story. If it is possible to have family worship twice a day, we would suggest some good devotional book to read for one of the periods. "Daily Light," a striking compilation of Scripture verses, with selected portions for morning and evening of each day of the year, is a fine handbook for family worship. Above all, the Bible should be read regularly.

Although it is often a struggle to find time for the family altar, it is one of those indispensable things for the Christian, and other duties must be sacrificed for it. You cannot have a real Christian home without having family worship. To try to do so will mean failure.

The problem, of course, is infinitely greater where there is a "divided family." But even if the head of the house is not a Christian, if he is willing for another member of the family to conduct family worship, either remaining present himself or withdrawing as he chooses, by all means, proceed with the family altar. It is an undisputed tragedy when the head of the house is opposed to family worship and will not tolerate it.

In such a case, the great challenge is to pray for his salvation. God works wonders in answer to earnest prayer.

It takes some determination to begin and carry on family worship faithfully, but the dividends are infinitely worth while. Actually, if I had to choose between family worship and public church worship, I would choose the former as having priority, for I believe that there is more blessing and spiritual strength imparted through family worship than there is in the church services.

No matter what the odds are or how hard it may be to maintain the family altar, carry it on at any cost. It is at the family altar where timid Christians in the family circle may first learn to pray. It is at the family altar where burdens may be freely poured out before the Lord, without fear or embarrassment. The family altar should be the very center of the Christian home, everything revolving around it and evolving from it.

Family life in a Christian home should pre-eminently be family worship. The home that has a regular family altar is a home that will not be shaken up or broken to pieces.

THE CHURCH

We would like to say a few words first regarding church membership. You should understand, of course, that church membership is not essential to salvation, nor is it a part of salvation. But we believe that church membership is a definite part of the Christian life and that every Christian should normally unite with some local church. Primarily, the church universal is a spiritual body, the Body of Christ, and every Christian is a member of that great organism. But that "spiritual" church is made up of hundreds and thousands of local congregations and assemblies all over the world. And for spiritual growth and help every Christian should unite and fellowship with one of the local churches. It will be a great aid to your spiritual life and growth if you do so.

Which church should one join? In reply to this question may we quote again from the venerable Dr. Torrey: "Unite with a church where they believe in the Bible and where they preach the Bible. Avoid the churches where words are spoken, open or veiled, that have a tendency to undermine your faith in the Bible as a reliable revelation from God himself, the all-sufficient rule of faith and practice. Unite with a church where there is a spirit of prayer, where the prayer meetings are well kept up. Unite with a church that has a real, active interest in the salvation of the lost, where young Christians are looked after and helped, where minister and people have a love for the poor and outcast, a church that regards its mission in this world to be the same as the mission of Christ, to seek and to save the lost.

"As to denominational differences, other things being equal, unite with that denomination whose ideas of doctrines and government and of the ordinances are most closely akin to your own. But it is better to unite with a live church of some other denomination than to unite with a dead church of your own. We live in a day when denominational differences are becoming ever less and less, and oftentimes they are of no practical consequence whatsoever; and one will often feel more at home in a church of some other denomination than in any accessible church of his own denomination. The things that divide the denominations are insignificant compared to the great fundamental truths and purposes and faith that unite them.

"If you cannot find a church that agrees with the patterns set forth above, find the church that comes nearest to it. Go into that church and by prayer and by work try to bring that church as nearly as you can to the pattern of what a church of Christ ought to be. But do not waste your strength in criticism against either church or minister. Seek that which is good in the church and in the minister and do your best to strengthen it. Hold aloof, firmly but unobtrusively, from what is wrong and seek to correct it. Do not be discouraged if you cannot correct it in a day or a week or a month or a year. Patient love and prayer and effort will tell in time. Drawing off by yourself and snarling and grumbling will do no good. That will simply make you and the truths for which you stand repulsive."

Here are some simple questions which you should ask concerning any church you may contemplate joining:

1. Is it true to the Bible? Does it hold the Bible to be the actual Word of God and uphold it as such in all the services?

2. Does the minister preach plainly concerning the atoning death of Christ on the cross, and does he emphasize His shed blood?

3. Do they preach "ye must be born again" positively?

4. Does the church have weekly prayer meetings? Do they actually pray at these prayer meetings?

5. Is there constant emphasis on the winning of souls, and are there real efforts in that direction?

6. Is the Holy Spirit's ministry recognized and emphasized in the preaching and the program of the church?

7. Does the ministry of the church hold forth the necessity of separation from the world and from worldly practices and amusements?

8. Do they have a foreign missionary program? Are they actively interested in missions? Are they giving to the support of missionaries and seeking to encourage their young people

to give their lives as missionaries?

9. Is the imminent return of Christ taught?

We believe that if all of these questions could be answered in the affirmative regarding any church, that church would be a splendid one to join. In case they cannot all be answered in the affirmative, make sure that at least the first six of them can. Do not join a church unless it holds to the inspiration of the Bible as God's Word, the necessity of the shed blood of Christ, the new birth, and true prayer.

Perhaps it is superfluous to say here that it is not merely enough to join a church. You must attend regularly. Do not get into the habit of attending church sporadically. Be regular in your attendance of worship in the house of God. Make a real effort to be there at least for the Sunday morning and evening services and at the midweek prayer meeting. Attend other services of the church as time and circumstances permit. By all means, attend the Sunday school regularly. If you positively cannot attend more services, let Sunday school, one Sunday service, and midweek prayer meeting be your absolute minimum. From that minimum you can expand your attendance to whatever program the church may have.

If you begin to neglect church attendance, you will probably drift in your own Christian life. If you habitually stay away from the house of God, you may become a real backslider. God, realizing the necessity of Christian fellowship in the church, has urged us not to forsake "the assembling of ourselves together" (Heb. 10:25). You need the inspiration that comes from united worship with other Christians. You need the strength that comes from the Word of God as it is preached from the pulpit. You need the inspiration that comes from fellowship with the other Christians in the church, so be regular in your attendance.

If you, as a Christian, are unfaithful in your attendance, it is a very bad testimony for your unsaved friends and neighbors. How can you expect them to go to church to hear the gospel preached, if you yourself, a Christian, are careless about it?

Not only should you join a church, not only should you attend a church, but you should participate in its activities and assume your share of the church's responsibilities. If you are qualified to fill any office in the church and are asked to do so, do it with a willing heart, as unto the Lord. If you are asked to teach a Sunday school class, teach it conscientiously and with all diligence. If you are requested to lead some group in the church, do so in the very best way you can, with the aid and help of God's Holy Spirit, prayerfully depending upon Him. If you are chosen to serve on some committee, even one that may deal with some of the more secular aspects of the church program, accept the responsibility honestly and do the best you can to carry out your duty. Do anything that you are asked to do in the church. Only decline when you conscientiously feel that you are unable to fill the position you are asked to take. Even then, pray about it before declining to accept the responsibility.

There are, of course, financial responsibilities that must accompany church membership, and you should expect to assume your part in those, too. There are expenses in connection with operating a church, and those expenses can only be met as the members give. So give to your church. Give liberally and give cheerfully, as unto the Lord. We shall say more about the matter of giving in the following chapter.

The church is the Christian's spiritual home while he is on earth. It is there that he is spiritually supported, comforted, and fitted for the society of heaven, where the entire family of God will at last assemble. It is there that he will cultivate fellowship with other saints of God. It is there that he makes his prayer burdens known to other members of God's family, who will mutually carry his burdens with him. It is there that he will turn for spiritual help in time of need and perhaps for material help also at times. It is there that he will be instructed in the Word of God and built up in the most holy faith. It is there that he will worship his God each Lord's Day in the beauty of His holiness and inquire in His temple.

Each individual Christian needs the fellowship of other believers. The outward expression of this fellowship is in the membership of some organized body of believers. If you hold aloof from all organized churches, hoping thus to have a broader fellowship with all believers belonging to all the churches, I fear that you will only deceive yourself. You will miss the helpfulness that comes from intimate union with a local congregation. Sometimes well-meaning persons have held aloof from church membership, but they usually have suffered in their spiritual life by doing so.

If you have really received the Lord Jesus Christ as your Saviour, hunt up, as soon as you can, some others who have received Him likewise and unite yourself with them in the church.

Bear in mind that you will not find a perfect church. If you wait until you find a perfect church before joining, you never will be able to join. If a church is true to the Word of God and the doctrines of the gospel of Jesus Christ, even though there may be some flaws in their conduct and practice, unite with them and do your part to contribute for the spiritual advancement of that church, and your own spiritual life will likewise be advanced.

We wish to say, however, before leaving this subject, that

it is better not to unite with a church at all than to unite with a modernistic church. By a "modernistic" church we mean a church that does not hold the Bible to be the Word of God and that does not consider the death of Christ as being essential to the salvation of sinners. Some churches do not preach the new birth, and they make no effort toward winning men and women to a personal acceptance of Jesus Christ. Most churches that are fundamental and spiritual will have a midweek prayer service, and that is one fairly good gauge by which you can tell the difference between a sound church and a modernistic church. In most communities in America, however, we dare say that there will be some church within your reach where you can have true Christian fellowship.

Chapter XIII

YOUR POCKETBOOK

Christian Stewardship

Was your pocketbook converted when you were converted? It should have been. If you have come to know and love the Lord, naturally it should be one of the desires of your heart to do whatever you can to further His cause in this world, not only by serving as you can, but by giving of your means to help others serve.

It is tragic that there are so many "unconverted" pocketbooks in Christians' garments! This is really difficult to understand, because one of the most common exercises of love is giving. When you love a person, you instinctively give gifts to that one. When a young fellow starts courting a girl, he begins to buy her candy and flowers and other gifts that he thinks will please her. At Christmas time we give gifts to the people who are near and dear to us; likewise, on their birthdays and other anniversaries. One of the most common ways in which love expresses itself is by the giving of gifts. It was because God so loved us that He gave to us the unspeakable gift, His only-begotten Son.

It is only natural that people who do not love God will not be interested in giving money to God's cause, but one who loves the Lord with all his heart surely will count it a duty and a privilege to give of his money to Christ's cause.

So if we really love God, we will desire to give Him some of our means.

The Bible has much to say about giving. During the Old Testament dispensation, the Dispensation of Law, God's people were required to give one tenth of all their increase to the Lord. This tithe was obligatory upon all, and in addition to the tithe, they were to add their "gifts."

Is tithing a binding law in the New Testament? Christians quite often raise this question. We do not personally hold that tithing is a law of the New Testament, but we certainly feel that the grace of God operating in a Christian today cannot expect less of us than did the law in Old Testament days. Since the law demanded a tithe of everything, grace does not ask less. In fact, grace ought to superabound far above and beyond the law. Really, some Christians, perhaps we should say many, ought to be ashamed of themselves for giving merely a tenth of what they have to the Lord. God has blessed them so abundantly that they should give far more, and yet they stick to the bare minimum of that which the Old Testament law required before the grace of God was fully revealed to men.

The rule of grace laid down in the New Testament is to give "as God hath prospered" (I Cor. 16:2). That entire verse reads, "Upon the first day of the week let every one of you lay by him in store, as God hath prospered him." There are two general principles laid down in this verse. One is to give regularly, "upon the first day of the week"; the other is to give according to your means, "as God hath prospered." There is no particular minimum requirement in the New Testament, nor is there a maximum limit. But every Christian should give according to the amount of money God has entrusted to him.

Another New Testament Scripture referring to giving is

II Corinthians 9:7, which reads, "Every man according as he purposeth in his heart, so let him give; not grudgingly, or of necessity: for God loveth a cheerful giver." And the verse just before this, verse 6, strikingly says, "But this I say, He which soweth sparingly shall reap also sparingly; and he which soweth bountifully shall reap also bountifully." The Lord Jesus said in Luke 6:38, "Give, and it shall be given unto you; good measure, pressed down, and shaken together, and running over, shall men give into your bosom. For with the same measure that ye mete withal it shall be measured to you again."

There seems to be a victorious circle pointed out here in giving. First, you give as God has prospered you. Secondly, as you give, God prospers you more, so that you can in turn give more, that you might be blessed again more, and so on! Christian friend, will you put this promise of God and law of grace to a test? Will you "prove" God by it?

Some friends were discussing a mutual acquaintance—a minister of the gospel. He is a loyal preacher of the Word of God, but for some reason he has always had an exceedingly difficult time financially. His financial problems seem to be quite in contrast to what one would naturally expect in the life of a man like him. As the reasons for this were discussed, one brother volunteered the information that perhaps this man had not been more blessed financially because he had always been so niggardly with his own money. He was a "pinch-penny preacher." There are many pinch-penny Christians, and the result is that they are spiritual paupers. Be a liberal Christian, and God will bless you liberally in return. He always does.

In the forty-seventh chapter of Ezekiel we have the record of one of Ezekiel's glorious visions from the Lord. In this vision he sees a river flowing out of the temple (a picture of God's grace), and an attending angel leads him into the water. He is led on by the angel farther and farther into the river, the water rising higher and higher on his body, until in the latter part of verse four we read, "The waters were to the loins." To me this is a picture of the Christian whose pockets have been immersed in the grace of God and have had a good dose of salvation, because pockets are always at the loins. What about you? Have you had your pockets submerged in the grace of God yet? Has your pocketbook been converted to Christ? Does the Spirit of God control your purse strings?

As we stated previously, we do not regard tithing as a law of the New Testament, but we believe that every Christian ought to have a regular plan for systematic giving. If you feel honestly before God that He does not expect you to give more than one tenth of your income, then be very careful to give at least the tithe to Him. Do it systematically. The best way is to put God's portion aside first when you get your pay check, or whatever form your income may take. It is a good plan to have in your home some container or special place for the "Lord's portion." Then put God's portion into it, first of all, and let it sacredly be regarded as no longer yours, but His. If you follow that plan, you will always have money to give when needs arise in the work of the Lord.

Evidently the Apostle Paul saw the value of systematic giving, and for that reason he pointed out that every man should, on the first day of the week, put aside his offering for the Lord. If you will put aside the Lord's portion weekly, you will find it much easier to give to God. It will become so habitual that you will never think of failing to give Him what you rightly should.

But beware of thinking that because you have given a

tenth, you have given all that God asks of you. Some Christians could give half of their income to the Lord, and they should. Some persons can give even a larger proportion. Remember that God looks not only at what you have given to Him, but also at what you have kept for yourself! God knows how much money you need to care for your family properly and meet your obligations. He knows, too, when you are spending money selfishly and foolishly. Self-ism is the very essence of sin, and if you have been saved from your sins, you must be weaned away from that sinful spirit. Your one desire in life, both in what you do and in what you earn, should be to glorify the name of Christ and further His work.

Some ministers strongly teach that all the money you give to God must be given to and through your local church. There is nothing in Scripture to establish this. We feel that this teaching arises largely from a kind of denominational parsimony. It is our personal conviction that it is a mistake to give all of one's money in one place. You should spread out your gifts, though not too thinly, so that you may have a share in God's work in various directions. Ministers who sponsor the teaching just referred to base it on Malachi 3:10, which says, "Bring ye all the tithes into the storehouse," making the church the present "storehouse." But this is a very farfetched interpretation of Scripture. The church is not like the Old Testament temple. The church has no storehouse and is not a storehouse. To mold the local church into this Old Testament verse has always seemed like dishonest Bible interpretation to me.

One should, of course, give liberally and regularly to the church to which he belongs. But we believe that the Christian should also give to other causes, particularly to some of the great interdenominational programs of God, such as gospel broadcasts, faith missions, etc. No pastor or Christian has a right to tell another Christian that he should not give money to these causes. The only time when one has a right to advise against giving money to any religious work is when that money is not being used to preach the gospel, or if the work is in some way not really true to Christ.

One needs to be very careful before giving his money to these programs outside the regular church, of course, for some of them are unreliable and unworthy. Careful investigation should be made. First of all, one should make certain that the organization is doctrinally sound. Secondly, one must make sure that it is financially sound. Any religious organization that is above board ought to send numbered receipts for all gifts given, and their books should be audited at least once a year and the auditor's report made available. If you desire to give money to a mission board or to support a missionary under some board, find out if the ones in charge are financially responsible, if they publish regular reports of all monies received, and if they have their books audited by Certified Public Accountants.

Do not give your money just because you are fascinated by some individual personality. Give your money to a person only as one of God's servants, because of what he is doing with it for the spreading of the gospel. Giving should never be for the purpose of lining the pockets of some favorite preacher, but always with a view to helping spread the testimony of Jesus Christ in a needy world.

Under no circumstances give your money, particularly missionary money, to modernistic organizations. If you belong to a church where the missionary program is modernistic, a church that sends out modernists to the mission field, do not give your money to that program. Give it to some other sound missionary organization. Not all denominational missionary boards are modernistic, by any means, but a number of them are. It was because of modernism in the older boards, and their loss of the pioneer spirit, that God raised up faith mission boards in our time.

If you have the right attitude toward your own redemption, you will have the right attitude toward Christian stewardship. If you have been redeemed, you belong to God, body and soul. In that case, all that you possess belongs to God, too—your physical strength, your mind, your personality, your possessions, and your money. The money that you have in your pocketbook and in your bank account is really God's money. It is only entrusted unto you as His steward. If you prove to be a poor steward, He may take it away from you and let it go into other hands.

You will have to give an account to God not only for the way you spent your time on earth as a Christian but also for the way you spent your money. If you spent it purely for selfish purposes or for modernistic or worldly enterprises, you will stand ashamed before your Saviour and be deprived of the reward which you could have had. Those who give to God's work (for instance, missionary work) will share in the rewards just as much as those who actually went out to the fields to gather in the harvest of souls.

If you are in a family where your partner is not a Christian, we realize that it is far more difficult for you to give to God's work. It is difficult for a Christian wife to give money to the Lord if her husband is unconverted and unwilling. But if you should be in that circumstance, it may still be possible for you to give out of the personal allowance that comes to you. Let the women of God, instead of spending their money on vain and worldly things, give it to the Lord. If Christian women who think that they cannot give anything to the Lord's work would spend as much money to make Christ attractive to people as they do in trying to make themselves attractive (whether they succeed or not is a question), they might be surprised at how much they could do.

Even little children who love the Lord should give Him a portion of the money they have, though it be but a few cents. If you are a Christian parent, teach your children diligently to give a portion of all the money that comes to them to the Lord. If they learn this habit in childhood, it will go with them through the years.

Once you have begun to give to God liberally, the blessings that you experience in your own soul as a result and the blessings that God will deliberately bring upon your life as a reward will so thrill you that giving will be one of your greatest joys. Remember, you cannot outgive God! The more you give to Him, the more He will give back to you. And the more He gives back to you, the more you can in turn give to Him again, as we pointed out previously. Join the triumphant circle of Christians who have learned to be stewards of God's blessings.

Chapter XIV

YOUR LIFE COMPANION

Choosing the Right One

One of the most serious questions in every Christian's life is that of choosing the right husband or wife. There is no step in which you need guidance more than at this point. It is a tragedy for a Christian young person to be united in marriage to one who will not walk together in agreement with him or her in the things of God. I have known numerous cases of this kind that have been positively heartbreaking.

Particularly is it a tragedy when one who has heard the call into some kind of Christian service marries a partner who will not go along with him in that service. Sometimes a life has had to be set aside completely from God's path and God's will because of an unwilling partner. In the Bible we read of Samson, a young man of God who missed God's richest blessings and spent the latter part of his life in misery and despair, because of uncontrolled affection for the wrong woman.

First of all, wait on God regarding your life's partner. Remember those familiar verses from the thirty-seventh Psalm, "Trust in the Lord, and do good . . . Delight thyself also in the Lord: and he shall give thee the desires of thine heart. Commit thy way unto the Lord; trust also in him; and he shall bring it to pass." This promise, of course, covers many problems in the Christian life, but it is an especially good promise to claim in the matter of choosing your helpmate. If you trust

God about the matter of a husband or wife, He will provide the right one for you. If your one desire and delight is to do the will of God, He will reward you by giving you a partner who will answer all the desires of your heart, who will love you dearly, whom you, in turn, will love purely. If you will commit your way unto the Lord and trust Him regarding this matter, "He shall bring it to pass."

Do not allow your natural affections or passions to cause you to jump over the traces in this matter and marry just any person who will stop for you or the one for whom you have set your cap, without praying and waiting upon God for guidance. Remember that marriage is a lifelong affair, not to be dissolved until God himself dissolves it by death. Divorce is not the will of God. It is an evil that ought not to be named among Christians. If you marry right in the first place, there will, of course, be no occasion for thinking about divorce. Obviously, when people are divorced, they are admitting that they made a mistake in marriage. But divorce is not the way out even for such a mistake. Divorce will only bring you a new set of problems, rather than solve the old ones.

One of my seminary professors, commenting on the matter of courtship and marriage, said, "Brethren, there is where you may make or break!" I have never forgotten it. When I look back to the companions of my student days, I realize that there were some who were made by marriage and others who were broken by their marriage.

What kind of a person should you marry? Perhaps you are facing this question right now. As a Christian, you can only consider marrying a person who meets certain qualifications. First of all, the one whom you marry must be a Christian. It cannot be the will of God for you to unite in marriage with a person who is not a Christian, no matter how much you might feel like doing so. The Bible says, "Be not unequally yoked together with unbelievers" (II Cor. 6:14). If you disregard this plain injunction from God, you will regret it in years to come. Under no circumstances allow yourself to propose marriage to or accept a proposal from one who is not saved.

Be firm in this determination. Make it clear to any person who is apparently in love with you that you will never consider marriage unless you are first united in Christ. Right here, though, you need to be cautious. Make sure that you do not cause that person to make just a sham profession of faith simply for the purpose of marrying you. You will no doubt be able to determine honestly whether he or she has genuinely come to know Christ or not. There are inevitable proofs in the life of everyone who is a real Christian. Do not marry a person with whom you cannot have prayer together before marriage, both of you taking part. If you follow that rule, you will never live to regret it.

Secondly, the one whom you marry must feel led into the same walk of life as you are. It is tragic for a Christian to be married to someone who, although he or she may be a Christian, refuses to walk together in the same chosen path. If a young man who is called to the ministry marries a girl who refuses to be a preacher's wife, he is in a sad predicament. If a girl who is called to the mission field marries a young man who wants to become an American businessman, she will have a sorrowful life. If God has called you to a certain type of work or a definite place of service, remember that He cannot lead you to marry someone who is called to some other kind of work in another place. God is never the author of confusion.

In the third place, there must be likemindedness regarding the ordinary things of life. Do not marry one whose likes and dislikes are completely opposite from yours. Only consider marriage to a person with whom you have a great many things in common. And this applies in a special way to spiritual matters. Have an understanding about which church you are going to belong to after you are married. There is nothing wrong in a Christian's marrying a person from a denomination other than his own, but let it be understood before marriage which church they will join. There must be likemindedness about that or there will be a divided family, and the children will suffer.

Ordinarily, in the case of Christians marrying from one denomination to another, the wife should sacrifice her denomination and join the church to which her husband belongs. But if the young man should belong to a church which is modernistic or unspiritual, the couple should decide between themselves beforehand either to join the church where the wife is, or, if desired, another church. Be reasonably sure that on major likes and dislikes and preferences there is some degree of likemindedness between the two of you before you join your entire earthly life to one another.

A proper marriage will result from a proper courtship. If the courtship is proper, honorably conducted, and prayerfully engaged in, it will not terminate in a mistaken marriage. If true godliness and piety are manifested by both toward each other during the time of courtship, there is not much danger of a shipwreck later. As young people date each other honorably and ethically, and as they pray and seek God's mind together regarding their future lives, the Lord will let them know whether or not they should become man and wife.

To you Christian young ladies, I would say that if a young man does not show true piety and morality toward you while he is courting you, remember that he will show less after you are married. Do not allow young men, although they may be professing Christians, to take improper liberties with you. "Necking" is "out" for Christians, in the sense that the world thinks of it. Even proper kissing and embracing should be refused until the time of engagement. Let the first kiss be experienced when the young man proposes to you, asking you to be his wife, and you, feeling led of God to do so, accept his proposal. Then, during the time of engagement, see that your courtship is limited to only decent embracing and kissing. No self-respecting Christian young man should fondle any of the private parts of a girl's body.

Young women, be careful with reference to clothing and posture, so that you will not make yourself a temptation and a prey to any young man. The way women, even including Christians, dress in these days, it is no wonder that men lose control of their passions and that there is so much sex transgression. A Christian young man might never be seriously tempted to commit a sex act with a strange woman, certainly not a harlot; but he might be put into a circumstance with the very girl he is courting and loves, so as to fall into fornication. Courtship is an important period in your life, so beware and watch your step.

A good rule for Christians who are courting each other would be to have prayer together every time they have a date. This would do more to keep you steady emotionally and morally than anything else in your whole experience.

Sex relationships before marriage are sinful under every circumstance. The Bible consistently terms this "fornication." Indulgence in such relations is not only contrary to the Word of God, but it also breaks down the proper affection and esteem that should exist between the man and woman after marriage. No man ever feels quite the same when he takes to the marriage altar a girl whose chastity he has already violated. No woman feels the same thrill in going to the marriage altar with a man with whom she has already had marriage relations. Their coming together following the marriage ceremony will never mean the same to either of them. The real thrill and deep joy of the marriage relationship has been marred and broken. It can never be the same as it otherwise would have been.

There is nothing sweeter or purer on this side of heaven than for two Christian young people, of like mind and like calling, to come to the marriage night together to give themselves wholly and purely over to each other. But there is nothing that is so likely to lead to distrust and bitterness in later life than for either of them to have violated their bodies by improper relationships before the time of marriage. It goes without saying, of course, that if a man and woman have fallen into fornication, there is nothing for them to do but be married at once. Then they must be loyal to each other for the rest of their lives. But the fact remains that such a marriage will never mean to either of them what it would have meant if they had both remained chaste.

Perhaps a further word should be spoken to young women. Sometimes girls are overly anxious to be married and, therefore, allow themselves to be carried off by anyone who will give them consideration. But to serious-minded Christian young ladies, I would like to quote the words spoken to me some years ago by a spinster. "I would rather be an old maid than wish I were one!" There is perhaps a touch of humor in this but also a heap of wisdom. If you cannot trust God to bring you a husband, you do not have faith enough to trust Him to help you live together with a man in a proper relationship after marriage. If God wants you to have a husband,

He will bring you one. If it should be His will for you to remain single for His sake, it certainly would be a tragedy for you to marry outside of His will. We believe that most cases of mistakes in marriages have been due to haste more than anything else. People are not willing to wait on God for their life partner. "Wait, I say, on the Lord."

Again I would caution Christian girls to be careful of the way they dress and conduct themselves, lest they make themselves a snare and a prey to evil men or a stumbling block to true Christian men. The craze for nudism that has swept our generation is of pagan origin. Nudism was once associated only with the heathen; now one sees it stalking the aisles of the church and invading the choir loft. Any girl who pays the price of separation from the world, who keeps her body properly clothed and maintains the complexion of skin that God has given her will, by a chaste and sincere waiting on God, one day be given a husband with whom she can dwell together in peace and blessedness, if it be God's will for her life.

A happy marriage and home is a foretaste of heaven. An unhappy marriage and home can be a miniature hell.

CHAPTER XV

PITFALLS TO AVOID

In closing this little book, we wish to point out some pitfalls to be avoided as you seek to walk with Christ. You may as well face the fact at the outset that there will be some stumbling along the way. No man has ever yet walked perfectly from the time of his conversion until he went home to meet the Lord. So if you do stumble, do not allow Satan to discourage you or to keep you down. Get up, confess your sins, ask for new grace, and press on! Press forward to the mark for the prize of the high calling of God in Jesus Christ.

Pitfall Number One: *Do not have your eyes too much on men.* David long ago said, "It is better to trust in the Lord than to put confidence in man" (Ps. 118:18). Numbers of young Christians have been discouraged because they had their eyes too much fixed upon some other Christian whom they considered to be almost perfect, and then when that Christian erred, they could not understand it. It is well to look up to other Christians, particularly older and stronger Christians, to receive help from them, but let us always remember that even the best Christian we know is only a human being, and he may bitterly disappoint us.

It is a serious blow when someone you have looked up to as being a real Christian, possibly a minister of the gospel, falls into sin; but if you have your eyes upon Jesus instead of upon a mere man, even though you will be disappointed by such experiences, you will not fall. The Apostle Paul said, "Let us lay aside every weight, and the sin which doth so easily beset us, and let us run with patience the race that is set before us, looking unto Jesus" (Heb. 12:1, 2). Some people are converted to a minister instead of to Christ. Such are candidates for a fall. As long as you keep your eyes on Jesus Christ, you will never be disappointed.

Pitfall Number Two: *Do not set your heart and desires too much on material things.* Remember, the Scriptures say, "The love of money is the root of all evil" (I Tim. 6:10). Paul, writing these words to young Timothy, further warned, "They that will be rich fall into temptation and a snare, and into many foolish and hurtful lusts" (v. 9). All through the Scriptures the danger of wealth and material prosperity is pointed out to the child of God, and Jesus frequently spoke of the difficulty a rich man would find in entering the kingdom of heaven. In explaining His parable about the seed and the sower to His disciples, He said. "The cares of this world, and the deceitfulness of riches, and the lusts of other things entering in, choke the word, and it becometh unfruitful" (Mark 4:19). Material riches are indeed "deceitful." The more one accumulates of the goods of this world, the more time he will want to spend accumulating still more.

Some Christians have been so taken up with the material side of life that they have neglected prayer, Bible-reading, church attendance, soul-winning, and every other spiritual activity. They are so busy "looking after their job." But behind what appears to be an innocent "looking after the job," there is that insatiable desire to accumulate the wealth of this world at any cost. In another place the Lord Jesus said, "Lay not up for yourselves treasures upon earth, were moth and rust doth corrupt, and where thieves break through and steal; but lay up for yourselves treasures in heaven" (Matt. 6:19, 20).

Whenever you feel the desire for money getting too much of a hold upon you, go to God in prayer and ask Him for victory over that desire. Have only one object in making money—to use it primarily for Christ's glory, utilizing only what you absolutely need for normal living expenses and the care of your family.

Pitfall Number Three: *Do not become intimate with unspiritual people.* We have spoken of companions in an earlier chapter, but may we just remind you again not to get too chummy with people who are earth-minded rather than Christ-minded. An unspiritual person, even though he may be a professing Christian, can drag you down spiritually and lead you far away from the straight and narrow path of the walk with God. Whenever you feel a person's influence upon you leading you away from Christ, make your association with that person less intimate.

Pitfall Number Four: *Do not fall into the habit of gossip and criticism.* Many Christians have ruined their spiritual lives by a bitter spirit. It is so easy to criticize and gossip, yet it is so detrimental to your own spiritual welfare. A minister of the gospel once said to me, "When I feel myself becoming critical, I just take a good square look at Jesus!"

Pitfall Number Five: *Beware of pride, conceit, and self-confidence.* In amplifying this, let me merely quote some statements from Scripture: "For I say, through the grace given unto me, to every man that is among you, not to think of himself more highly than he ought to think" (Rom. 12:3). "Humble yourselves in the sight of the Lord, and he shall lift you up" (Jas. 4:10). "Pride goeth before destruction, and an haughty spirit before a fall" (Prov. 16:18). "An high look, and a proud heart, and the plowing of the wicked, is sin" (Prov. 21:4). "Let him that thinketh he standeth take heed lest he fall" (I Cor. 10:12). "God resisteth the proud, but giveth grace unto the humble. Submit yourselves therefore to God" (Jas. 4:6).

Here is a final word of exhortation and encouragement: "Therefore, my beloved brethren, be ye steadfast, unmoveable, always abounding in the work of the Lord, forasmuch as ye know that your labour is not in vain in the Lord."